EASY
FRENCH
PHRASE
BOOK

NEW EDITION

Over 700 Phrases
for Everyday Use

Heather McCoy, Ph.D.

DOVER PUBLICATIONS, INC.
Mineola, New York

Bibliographical Note

Easy French Phrase Book NEW EDITION: Over 700 Phrases for Everyday Use,
first published by Dover Publications, Inc., in 2012, is a new selection of
material from *1001 Easy French Phrases,* published in 2010 by
Dover Publications, Inc.

Library of Congress Cataloging-in-Publication Data

McCoy, Heather.
  Easy French phrase book : new edition : over 700 phrases for everyday use /
Heather McCoy. — New ed.
    p. cm.
  Text in English and French.
  ISBN-13: 978-0-486-49902-4
  ISBN-10: 0-486-49902-2
  1. French language—Conversation and phrase books—English. I. Title.

PC2121.M55 2012
448.3'421—dc23

                                                          2012019698

Manufactured in the United States by LSC Communications
49902203   2017
www.doverpublications.com

Table of Contents

Introduction

This book is designed for the traveler or casual user of French who is looking for a handy and manageable guide to basic French phrases. The phrases included in this convenient volume are some of the basic tools for communication and comprehension that you are likely to need in a variety of French-speaking contexts.

The primary focus of *Easy French Phrase Book NEW EDITION* is daily communication. You will find linguistic structures that focus on describing yourself and others; asking simple questions that one might need when traveling; and interacting in a variety of situations. The phrases have been organized thematically so that you can easily find vocabulary and sentence structures that apply to a specific context. Special attention has been paid to organizing phrases so that you can substitute the vocabulary you need in order to create your own meaning, such as in the following example:

"Je voudrais prendre . . ." *(I'd like to have . . .)*
  une bière (a beer)
  un café (a coffee)

You will be able to use this book in a variety of ways, either by preparing for a trip by reading a few sections a day, or by using it on-the-spot by flipping to the section that is most pertinent at that moment. Our hope is that you will find the phrases useful and flexible, enabling you to effectively create your own meanings.

French Pronunciation

Easy French Phrase Book NEW EDITION uses a phonetic transcription as an aid to correct pronunciation. (See "Scheme of Pronunciation," below.) This transcription is located directly beneath the French entry in the text. Here are some general principles of pronunciation:

Nasalization

In French, a vowel is nasalized when it is followed by a single *m* or *n* in the same syllable. The transcription of these nasalized vowels appears as:

-an, -am, -em, -en -> ahn, ehn
-in, -im -> ihn, ihm
-on, -om -> ohn, ohm
-um, -un -> uhn

To produce a nasalized vowel, quickly pass the air through both the nose and the mouth at the same time. The *m* or *n* isn't pronounced after the nasal vowel, as follows:

français -> frahn-say; *temps* -> tahn
pain -> pihn; *printemps* -> prihn-tehn
bon -> bohn
quelqu'un -> kell-kuhn

Silent Final Consonants

In French, most consonants at the end of a word are silent, although there are exceptions to this rule: *c*, *f*, and *l*. The consonant *r* also is pronounced, but is silent when occurring in the endings *-er* and *-ier*.

The French r

The French *r* can be one of the most challenging sounds for English speakers to pronounce. Pronunciation of the *r* will depend upon the region of the French-speaking world that you are visiting. In some areas, the French *r* can resemble the Italian or Spanish *r*—produced by rolling it on the tip of the tongue. The Parisian *r* is a more gutteral sound: it's helpful to imagine the sound being produced in the back of the throat, the same place that produces the *h* in "ahoy." The *r* is voiced, meaning that there is a slight vibration of the vocal cords.

The Plural s

As mentioned above, consonants at the end of words normally are not pronounced. Make special note of this when pronouncing the *s* that denotes the plural:

Le chat -> luh-shah
Les chats -> lay-shah

Notice how the pronunciation of the noun *chat* does not change between the singular and the plural. This is quite different from English, and is important for English speakers to remember.

Liaison

A final consonant that is normally silent is pronounced when it comes before a vowel or *h*. This phenomenon is called *liaison*. Note the following change:

A final *s* before a consonant: *des livres* -> day-leev-ruh
A final *s* before a vowel: *des animaux* -> daze-ehn-ee-moh

The rules for liaison can be somewhat complex, so simply pay attention to the phonetic transcriptions in order to get a feel for when its usage is appropriate.

Stress

The last syllable of a French word is usually stressed:

Beaucoup -> boh-<u>koo</u>

However, when the last syllable is an unstressed *e* (*uh* in the transcription used here), the next-to-the-last syllable receives the stress:

Formidable -> for-mee-<u>dah</u>-bluh

You will also notice that in addition to the stress at the end of a word, there also is stress at the end of a phrase:

Je suis américain et travaille au musée d'art contemporain. -> zhuh swee <u>za</u>-mary-<u>kihn</u> ay tra-vy oh moo-<u>zay</u> <u>dar</u> cohn-<u>tehn</u>-por-<u>ihn</u>.

Scheme of Pronunciation

Letters	Transcription	Example	Notes
a	a	as in *ask*, but cut short	
	ah	as in *father*	
ai	ay	as in *play*	
	y	as in *why*	
au	oh	as in *bow*	See note on *o* below.
b	b	as in *bear*	
c	k	as in *car*	Pronounced *k* before *a*, *o*, or *u*
	s	as in *sun*	Pronounced *s* before *e* and *i*
ç	s	as in *sun*	
d	d	as in *danger*	Formed by touching tongue tip to teeth
e, è	eh	as in *met*	
é	ay	as in *play*	
e, eu, œu	uh	as in *bubble*	
f	f	as in *fan*	
g	g	as in *give*	Before *a*, *o*, and *u*
g	zh	as in *garage*	Before *e* and *i*
gn	ny	as in *canyon*	
h	silent		
i	ee	as in *feet*	
j	zh	as in *garage*	
k	k	as in *kernel*	

l	l	as in *lap*	
m	m	as in *me*	
n	n	as in *note*	
o	oh	as in *toe*	
oi	wa	as in *want*	
ou	oo	as in *boom*	
p	p	as in *pat*	
ph	f	as in *fan*	
q	k	as in *kernel*	
r	r	as in *red*	See section above.
s	ss	as in *lass*	At the beginning of the word or when doubled
	z	as in *zap*	When between two vowels
	silent		At the end of a word, unless followed by a vowel. See section above.
t	t	as in *tip*	
th	t	as in *tip*	
u	oo	no English equivalent	Formed by saying "ee," moving lips into rounded position without moving tongue.
v	v	as in *vote*	
w	v, w	as in *vote, win*	
x	ks	as in *licks*	
y	ee	as in *greet*	
z	z	as in *zoo*	

EASY
FRENCH
PHRASE
BOOK

NEW EDITION

Chapter 1
Greetings and Everyday Expressions

GREETINGS, INTRODUCTIONS, AND SOCIAL CONVERSATION

One of the ways in which French differs from English is that French uses formal and informal registers of language. These are expressed in the choice of the subject pronoun (*vous* is formal; *tu* is informal); the form of the verb; and, sometimes, in the way a question is formed. Always address adults whom you don't know well using the formal form of the verb, and reserve the informal for friends and children. It is interesting to note that Americans have a tendency to be informal in many situations in which the French prefer to interact formally. We've indicated below whenever a given sentence is formal or informal.

You will discover that although the subject pronoun for "we" is *nous,* the pronoun *on* frequently is used instead. You can usually tell by the context whether the speaker using *on* is referring to someone in general, or to the first-personal plural form "we."

You also will note that another difference between French and English is that nouns in French are either masculine or feminine. This has nothing to do with actual gender—say, the inherent masculine nature of *le stylo* (the pen), so it's better to memorize the gender of a noun rather than try to figure out this system of classification! Another important aspect to remember about the gender of nouns in French is that articles, adjectives, pronouns, and some verbs must agree with nouns in gender and number. We have indicated this below where appropriate by providing both the masculine and feminine forms, with the feminine form indicated either with an "e" in parentheses or given in a separate example. Note that when choosing sentences to describe yourself, you'll want to choose the appropriate form.

1. Good morning.   *Bonjour.*   **Bohn-zhoor**

2. Good evening.   *Bonsoir.*   **Bohn-swahr**

3. Good night. (bedtime)   *Bonne nuit.*   **Buhn nwee**

4. Hello.   *Bonjour.*   **Bohn-zhoor**

5. Hi.   *Salut.*   **Sah-loo**

6. Good-bye.   *Au revoir.*   **Oh ruh vwahr**

7. See you soon.   *À bientôt.*   **Ah byehn-toh**

8. Have a nice day.   *Bonne journée.*   **Buhn zhoor-nay**

9. My name is . . .   *Je m'appelle . . .*   **Zhuh ma-pel**

10. Allow me to introduce you to . . . (most formal)
    Permettez-moi de vous présenter . . .
    Per-meh-tay mwah duh voo pray-zehn-tay

my colleagues.	*mes collègues.*	**may koll-eg**
my friend. (m—masculine)	*mon ami.*	**mohn ah-mee**
my friend. (f—feminine)	*mon amie.*	**mohn ah-mee**

11. This is . . . (formal)   *Je vous présente . . .*
    Zhuh voo pray-zehnt

my wife.	*ma femme.*	**ma fahm**
my husband.	*mon mari.*	**mohn mah-ree**
my spouse/partner.	*mon conjoint.*	**mohn kon-zhwehn**
my boyfriend.	*mon copain.*	**mohn co-pihn**
my girlfriend.	*ma copine.*	**ma co-peen**

12. This is . . . (informal)   *Voici . . .*   **Vwa-see**

my daughter.	*ma fille.*	**ma fee**
my son.	*mon fils.*	**mohn feese**
my child.	*mon enfant.*	**mohn ehn-fehn**
my children.	*mes enfants.*	**maze ehn-fehn**
my brother.	*mon frère.*	**mohn fraire**

my sister.   *ma sœur.*   ma suhr

my family.   *ma famille.*   ma <u>fa</u>-mee

13. Pleased to meet you.
    Enchanté. (if you are male)   Enchantée. (if you are female)
    Ehn-<u>shehn</u>-tay

14. What line of work are you in?   *Quelle est votre profession?*
    Kell ay <u>vote</u> pro-fess-yion

15. I am . . .   *Je suis . . .*   <u>Zhuh</u> swee

    a stay-at-home mom.   *femme au foyer.*   **fahm oh-<u>fwa</u>-yay**

    a doctor.   *médecin.*   <u>**made**</u>**-sihn**

    a teacher.   *prof.*   **prohf**

    a university professor.   *un(e) universitaire.*
    uhn / oon oo-<u>nee</u>-vers-uh-<u>tare</u>

    a businessman.   *homme d'affaires.*   **umm <u>dah</u>-fare**

    a businesswoman.   *femme d'affaires.*   **fahm <u>dah</u>-fare**

    an architect.   *architecte.*   **are-<u>shee</u>-tekt**

    an engineer.   *ingénieur.*   **ihn-<u>zhayn</u>-yer**

    a scientist.   *un(e) scientifique.*   **uhn / oon see-<u>yehn</u>-tee-feek**

16. I am retired.   *Je suis à la retraite.*
    Zhuh swee ah la <u>ruh</u>-tret

17. I'm a college student.   *Je suis étudiant(e).*
    Zhuh swee zay-too-<u>dyehn</u>   Zhuh swee zay-too-<u>dyehnt</u>

18. I'm studying . . .   *J'étudie . . .*   **Zhay-too-<u>dee</u>**

    English.   *l'anglais.*   **lehn-<u>glay</u>**

    history.   *l'histoire.*   **lee-<u>stwahre</u>**

    French.   *le français.*   **luh frehn-<u>say</u>**

    biology.   *la biologie.*   **la <u>bee-oh</u>-low-zhee**

    chemistry.   *la chimie.*   **la <u>shee</u>-mee**

    engineering.   *l'ingénierie.*   **lihn-<u>zhayn</u>-yoor-ee**

19. How are you? (formal)   *Comment allez-vous?*
    <u>**Kuh-muh**</u> **tall-ay voo**

20. How are you? (informal)   *Ça va?*   **Sah <u>vah</u>**

21. Fine, thanks. And you?   *Je vais bien, merci. Et vous? (formal)*
     Je vais bien, merci. Et toi? (informal)
     Zhuh vay <u>byehn</u> mare-see. Ay voo
     Zhuh vay <u>byehn</u> mare-see. Ay twah

22. All right.   *Ça va.*   **Sah <u>vah</u>**

23. Where are you from? (formal)   *D'où venez-vous?*
     Doo vuh-nay <u>voo</u>

24. Where are you from? (informal)   *Tu viens d'où?*
     Too vyihn <u>doo</u>

25. I am from Boston.   *Je suis de Boston.*
     Zhuh swee duh bos-ton

26. I am American.
     Je suis américain. (m.)   Je suis américaine. (f.)
     Zhuh swee za-mary-<u>kihn</u>   Zhuh swee za-mary-<u>kenn</u>

27. Are you French?
     Vous êtes français? (m.)   Vous êtes française? (f.)
     Voo zet frehn-<u>say</u>   Voo zet frehn-<u>sez</u>

28. What a pleasure to see you.
     Quel plaisir de vous voir. (formal and when addressing a group)
     Quel plaisir de te voir. (informal)
     Kell play-zeer duh voo <u>vwahr</u>   Kell play-zeer duh tuh <u>vwahr</u>

29. Come visit us.   *Venez nous rendre visite.*
     Vuh-nay noo rand-ruh <u>vee-zeet</u>

30. Can I visit you sometime? (informal)
     Je peux te rendre visite un jour?
     Zhuh puh tuh rand-ruh <u>vee-zeet</u> uhn zhoor

31. What is your address?
     Quelle est votre adresse? (formal)
     Quelle est ton adresse? (informal)
     Kell ay vote ah-<u>dress</u>   Kell ay tone ah-<u>dress</u>

32. What is your phone number?
    Quel est votre numéro de téléphone? (formal)
    Quel est ton numéro de téléphone? (informal)
    Kell ay vote noo-mare-<u>oh</u> duh tay-lay-<u>phone</u>
    Kell ay tone noo-mare-<u>oh</u> duh tay-lay-<u>phone</u>

33. What is your email address?
    Quelle est votre adresse courriel? (formal)
    Quelle est ton adresse courriel? (informal)
    Kell ay vote ah-<u>dress</u> koo-ree-ehl
    Kell ay tone ah-<u>dress</u> koo-ree-ehl

34. Here is my address.   *Voici mon adresse.*
    Vwa-see mohn ah-<u>dress</u>

35. Here is my cellphone number.
    Voici mon numéro de portable.
    Vwa-see mohn noo-mare-<u>oh</u> duh por-<u>tahble</u>

36. Here is my website address.
    Voici l'adresse de mon site Internet.
    Vwa-see lah-<u>dress</u> duh mohn seet In-tare-<u>net</u>

37. May I see you again?   *Puis-je vous revoir?*
    <u>Pwee</u>-zhuh voo ruh-<u>vwahr</u>

MAKING YOURSELF UNDERSTOOD

When approaching a stranger to ask a question, remember to show politeness by starting with *"Excusez-moi, Madame"* when addressing a woman and *"Excusez-moi, Monsieur"* when addressing a man.

38. Do you speak English?
    Vous parlez anglais? (formal)
    Tu parles anglais? (informal)
    Voo pah-lay ehn-<u>glay</u>   Too pahl ehn-<u>glay</u>

39. Does anyone here speak English?
    Il y a quelqu'un qui parle anglais ici?
    Eel ya <u>kell-kuhn</u> kee pahl ehn-glay <u>ee-see</u>

40. I speak a little French.   *Je parle un peu français.*
    <u>Zhuh</u> pahl uhn <u>puh</u> frehn-say

41. I speak only English.   *Je ne parle que l'anglais.*
    <u>Zhuh</u> nuh pahl <u>kuh</u> lehn-<u>glay</u>

42. I don't speak French well.   *Je ne parle pas bien français.*
    <u>Zhuh</u> nuh pahl pah <u>byehn</u> frehn-say

43. Can you translate this word?   *Pouvez-vous traduire ce mot?*
    Poo-vay voo <u>trah</u>-dweer suh <u>moh</u>

44. Do you understand?   *Vous comprenez?*   <u>Voo</u> com-pren-<u>ay</u>

45. I understand.   *Je comprends.*   <u>Zhuh</u> kom-<u>prehn</u>

46. I don't understand.   *Je ne comprends pas.*
    Zhuh nuh <u>kom-prehn</u> pah

47. Say it again, please.   *Répétez, s'il vous plaît.*
    Ray-pay-<u>tay</u> see voo <u>play</u>

48. Speak more slowly, please.
    Parlez moins vite, s'il vous plaît.
    Pah-lay <u>mwehn veet</u> see voo <u>play</u>

49. Write it down, please.   *Pouvez-vous l'écrire, s'il vous plaît?*
    Poo-vay voo <u>lay-kreer</u> see voo <u>play</u>

50. How do you say "dog" in French?
    Comment dit-on "dog" en français?
    Kuh-muh <u>dee-ton</u> dog ehn frehn-<u>say</u>

51. What does this mean in English?
    Que veut dire cela en anglais?
    Kuh vuh deer suh-<u>lah</u> ehn ehn-<u>glay</u>

USEFUL WORDS AND EXPRESSIONS

52. Yes.   *Oui.*   **Wee**

53. No.   *Non.*   **Noh**

54. Maybe.   *Peut-être.*   **Puh <u>tet</u>-ruh**

55. Please.   *S'il vous plaît. (formal)*   *S'il te plaît. (informal)*
    See voo <u>play</u>   Seel tuh <u>play</u>

56. Thanks (a lot).   *Merci (beaucoup).*   <u>Mare</u>-see (<u>boh</u>-koo)

57. You're welcome. (formal)   *Je vous en prie.*
    Zhuh voo <u>zehn</u> pree

58. You're welcome. (informal)   *De rien.*   <u>Duh</u> ree-ehn

59. Pardon?   *Pardon?*   Par-<u>duhn</u>

60. Excuse me! (to get someone's attention)   *Excusez-moi!*
    Ecks-<u>kyoo-zay</u> mwah

61. Can I help you?   *Je peux vous aider?*
    Zhuh poo <u>vooz</u> ay-day

62. Please come in.   *Entrez, s'il vous plaît. (formal)*
    Entre, s'il te plaît. (informal)
    <u>Ehn</u>-tray see voo play   <u>Ehn</u>-tray seel tuh play

63. Come here.
    Venez, s'il vous plaît. (formal)   Viens, s'il te plaît. (informal)
    <u>Vuh</u>-nay see voo play   Vyihn seel tuh play

64. I am in a hurry.   *Je suis pressé. (m.)   Je suis pressée. (f.)*
    Zhuh swee <u>press</u>-say   Zhuh swee <u>press</u>-say

65. I am late.   *Je suis en retard.*   Zhuh swee ehn <u>ruh</u>-tar

66. I am hungry.   *J'ai faim.*   Zhay <u>fihm</u>

67. I am thirsty.   *J'ai soif.*   Zhay <u>swahf</u>

68. I am tired.   *Je suis fatigué. (m.)   Je suis fatiguée. (f.)*
    Zhuh swee fah-tee-<u>gay</u>   Zhuh swee fah-tee-<u>gay</u>

69. What's wrong?   *Qu'est-qu'il y a?*   Kess keel <u>yah</u>

70. It's ok.   *Ça va.*   Sah <u>vah</u>

71. I know.   *Je sais.*   Zhuh say

72. I don't know.   *Je ne sais pas.*   Zhuh nuh say <u>pah</u>

73. It doesn't matter.   *Ça ne fait rien.*   Sah nuh fay ree-<u>ehn</u>

74. It's not serious.   *C'est pas grave.*   Say pah <u>grahv</u>

75. Can you help me?   *Vous pouvez m'aider?*
Voo poo-vay <u>may-day</u>

76. Where is the restroom?   *Où sont les toilettes?*
Oo sone lay twah-<u>let</u>

77. Leave me alone!   *Laissez-moi tranquille!*
Lay-say mwah tran-<u>kee</u>

78. I am looking for . . .   *Je cherche . . .*   **Zhuh <u>share-sh</u>**
    my hotel.   *mon hôtel.*   **mohn oh-<u>tell</u>**
    the train station.   *la gare.*   **lah gahr**
    a restaurant.   *un restaurant.*   **uhn ress-toh-<u>rehn</u>**
    a bank.   *une banque.*   **oon <u>behn</u>-kuh**

79. Who?   *Qui?*   **Kee**

80. What?   *Quoi?*   **Kwah**

81. Why?   *Pourquoi?*   **Por-<u>kwah</u>**

82. Where?   *Où?*   **Oo**

83. When?   *Quand?*   **Kehn**

84. How much?   *Combien?*   **Kum-<u>byehn</u>**

85. How long/much time?   *Combien de temps?*
Kum-<u>byehn</u> duh <u>tehn</u>

86. To.   *À.*   **Ah**

87. From.   *De.*   **Duh**

88. With.   *Avec.*   **Ah-<u>vek</u>**

89. Without.   *Sans.*   **Sehn**

90. In.   *Dans.*   **Dehn**

91. On.   *Sur.*   **Soor**

92. Near.   *Près de.*   **Pray duh**

93. Far.   *Loin de.*   **Lwehn duh**

94. In front of. *Devant.* **Duh-vehn**

95. Behind. *Derrière.* **Dare-ee-air**

96. Next to. *À côté de.* **Ah koh-tay duh**

97. Outside. *À l'extérieur.* **Ah lecks-tare-ee-er**

98. Inside. *À l'intérieur.* **Ah lehn-tare-ee-er**

99. Empty. *Vide.* **Veed**

100. Full. *Plein. (m.) Pleine. (f.)* **Plihn   Plen**

101. Something. *Quelque chose.* **Kell-kuh shows**

102. Nothing. *Rien.* **Ree-ehn**

103. Several. *Plusieurs.* **Ploo-zyer**

104. (Much) more. *(Beaucoup) plus.* **(Boh-koo) ploos**

105. Less. *Moins.* **Mwehn**

106. (A little) more. *(Un peu) plus.* **(Uhn puh) ploos**

107. Enough. *Assez.* **ah-say**

108. Too much. *Trop.* **Troh**

109. Look out! *Attention!* **Ah-tehn-syion**

110. Listen! *Écoutez!* **Ay-koo-tay**

DESCRIBING YOURSELF AND OTHERS

111. What does he look like? *Comment est-il?* **Kuh-muh et eel**

112. Can you describe him/her? *Pouvez-vous le / la décrire?*
Poo-vay-voo luh / lah day-kreer

113. He is young / old. *Il est jeune / vieux.*
Eel ay zhuhn / vee-yuh

114. She is (quite) young / old. *Elle est (très) jeune / vielle.*
Ell ay (tray) zhun / vee-yay

115. He has . . . eyes.   *Il a les yeux . . .*   Eel ah lays yuh . . .

blue.	*bleus.*	<u>bluh</u>
green.	*verts.*	<u>vair</u>
brown.	*marron.*	mah-<u>ruhn</u>
hazel.	*noisette.*	<u>nwah</u>-zet
gray.	*gris.*	<u>gree</u>

116. She has . . . hair.   *Elle a les cheveux . . .*
Ell ah lay shuh-vuh . . .

brown.	*bruns.*	<u>bruhn</u>
gray.	*gris.*	<u>gree</u>
blond.	*blonds.*	<u>blohn</u>
red.	*roux.*	<u>roo</u>

117. He has . . . hair.   *Il a des cheveux . . .*
Eel ah day shuh-vuh

short.	*courts.*	<u>koor</u>
long.	*longs.*	<u>lohn</u>
straight.	*raides.*	<u>red</u>
curly.	*bouclés.*	boo-<u>klay</u>

118. He's bald.   *Il est chauve.*   Eel ay <u>shoh</u>-vuh

119. He has a beard and a mustache.
Il porte une barbe et une moustache.
Eel port oon <u>barb</u> ay oon moo-<u>stash</u>

120. I am . . .   *Je suis . . .*   Zhuh swee . . .

tall.	*grand(e).*	<u>grehn</u> / <u>grehn</u>-duh
short.	*petit (e).*	<u>puh-tee</u> / <u>puh-teet</u>
(very) thin.	*(très) mince.*	(tray) <u>mihnse</u>
(not very) fat.	*(pas très) gros(se).*	(pah tray) <u>grow</u> / <u>gross</u>

DIFFICULTIES

121. I cannot find my hotel address.
Je ne peux pas trouver l'adresse de mon hôtel.
Zhuh nuh puh pah troo-vay lah-<u>dress</u> duh mohn oh-<u>tell</u>

122. Can you help me?   *Vous pouvez m'aider?*
     Voo poo-vay <u>may-day</u>

123. Help! (in case of an emergency)   *Au secours!*
     Oh <u>suh-koor</u>

124. I have lost . . .   *J'ai perdu . . .*   **Zhay pair-<u>doo</u>**
     my keys.   *mes clés.*   **may klay**
     my passport.   *mon passeport.*   **mohn <u>pass</u>-pore**
     my wallet.   *mon portefeuille.*   **mohn <u>por</u>-tuh-foy**
     my purse.   *mon sac à main.*   **mohn <u>sak</u>-ah-man**
     my ticket.   *mon billet.*   **mohn <u>bee</u>-yay**

125. Have you seen . . . ?   *Avez-vous vu . . . ?*   **Ah-vay voo <u>vooh</u>**
     my husband   *mon mari*   **mohn mah-<u>ree</u>**
     my wife   *ma femme*   **mah <u>fahm</u>**

126. I forgot my money.   *J'ai oublié mon argent.*
     Zhay oo-blee-yay mohn <u>ar</u>-zhehn

127. I have missed my train.   *J'ai manqué mon train.*
     Zhay mehn-kay mohn <u>trehn</u>

128. What should I do?   *Que dois-je faire?*
     Kuh dwah-zhuh <u>fair</u>

129. Can you help me contact . . . ?
     Pouvez-vous m'aider à contacter . . . ?
     Poo-vay voo may-day ah <u>kone</u>-tahk-tay
     my famille   *ma famille*   **mah fah-<u>mee</u>**
     my colleague   *mon (m.) / ma (f.) collègue*
     mohn <u>koll</u>-eg   mah <u>koll</u>-eg

130. My glasses are broken.   *Mes lunettes sont cassées.*
     May loo-net sohn <u>ka</u>-say

131. Where can I get them repaired?   *Où peut-on les faire réparer?*
     Oo puh-tuhn lay fair <u>ray</u>-pah-<u>ray</u>

132. I need a new hearing aid.
J'ai besoin d'un nouvel appareil acoustique.
Zhay buh-zwehn duhn noo-vell <u>ah</u>-pah-ray <u>ah-koo</u>-steek

133. This is my medication.   *Voici mes médicaments.*
Vwa-see may <u>may-dee</u>-kah-<u>mehn</u>

134. Where is the lost-and-found desk?
Où se trouve le bureau des objets trouvés?
Oo suh troov luh <u>boo</u>-roh daze <u>ub-zhay</u> troo-<u>vay</u>

135. Is the American consulate nearby?
Est-ce que le consulat des États-Unis est près d'ici?
Ess kuh luh kone-suh-<u>lah</u> daze ay-tahz ay oo-<u>nee</u> pray dee-<u>see</u>

136. I'm looking for the police station.
Je cherche la station de police.
Zhuh <u>share-sh</u> lah stah-<u>see-yion</u> duh <u>poh</u>-lees

137. I am going to call a policeman.
Je vais appeler un agent de police.
Zhuh vaze <u>ah</u>-pull-<u>ay</u> uhn azh-ehn duh <u>poh</u>-lees

NUMBERS AND TELLING TIME

In France and most other French-speaking countries, the 24-hour clock, or *l'heure officielle*, is used for transportation schedules as well as other official situations. Seven o'clock in the morning would be written in *l'heure conventionnelle* as 7h00, whereas seven o'clock at night would be 19h00. An easy way to convert from the 24-hour clock to the American convention of telling time is to subtract 12.

138. One.   *Un.*   Uhn

139. Two.   *Deux.*   Duh

140. Three.   *Trois.*   Twah

141. Four.   *Quatre.*   Kaht

142. Five.   *Cinq.*   Sank

143. Six.   *Six.*   Sees

144. Seven. *Sept*. **Set**

145. Eight. *Huit*. **Weet**

146. Nine. *Neuf*. **Nuff**

147. Ten. *Dix*. **Dees**

148. Eleven. *Onze*. **Ownz**

149. Twelve. *Douze*. **Dooz**

150. Thirteen. *Treize*. **Trayze**

151. Fourteen. *Quatorze*. **Kah-torze**

152. Fifteen. *Quinze*. **Kehnze**

153. Sixteen. *Seize*. **Sez**

154. Seventeen. *Dix-sept*. **Dee-set**

155. Eighteen. *Dix-huit*. **Dee-zweet**

156. Nineteen. *Dix-neuf*. **Dee-znuff**

157. Twenty. *Vingt*. **Vihn**

158. Twenty-one. *Vingt-et-un*. **Vihn-tay-uhn**

159. Twenty-two. *Vingt-deux*. **Vihn-duh**

160. What time is it? *Quelle heure est-il?* **Kell er et eel**

161. It is seven o'clock. *Il est sept heures*. **Eel ay set er**

162. It is nine o'clock in the morning.
      Il est neuf heures du matin. **Eel ay nuff er doo ma-tan**

163. Is it three-thirty? *Il est trois heures et demie?*
      Eel ay twa zer ay duh-mee

164. No, it's three forty-five.
      Non, il est quatre heures moins le quart.
      Noh eel ay kaht rer mwehn luh kar

165. It's noon.   *Il est midi.*   **Eel ay <u>mee</u>-dee**

166. It's midnight.   *Il est minuit.*   **Eel ay <u>mee</u>-nwee**

167. My train is at a quarter to ten.
Mon train part à dix heures moins dix.
Mohn trehn par ah <u>dee</u> <u>zer</u> mwehn dees

168. At ten minutes past seven.   *À sept heures dix.*
Ah <u>set</u> er dees

TALKING ABOUT DAYS OF THE WEEK AND MONTHS

169. Today.   *Aujourd'hui.*   **Oh-zhoor-<u>dwee</u>**

170. Tomorrow.   *Demain.*   **Duh-<u>mihn</u>**

171. Yesterday.   *Hier.*   **Ee-<u>yair</u>**

172. Week.   *Semaine.*   **Suh-<u>men</u>**

173. Next week.   *La semaine prochaine.*
Lah suh-<u>men</u> pro-<u>shen</u>

174. Last week.   *La semaine dernière.*   **Lah <u>suh-men</u> dare-nyair**

175. See you next week!   *À la semaine prochaine!*
Ah lah suh-<u>men</u> pro-<u>shen</u>

176. Day.   *Le jour.*   **Luh zhoor**

177. Month.   *Le mois.*   **Luh mwah**

178. Year.   *L'année.*   **Lah-<u>nay</u>**

179. Next year.   *L'année prochaine.*   **Lah-<u>nay</u> pro-<u>shen</u>**

180. Last year.   *L'année dernière.*   **Lah-<u>nay</u> dare-<u>ny</u>air**

181. What day is it today?   *Quel jour sommes-nous?*
Kell zhoor <u>summ</u> noo

182. I work on ...   *Je travaille ...*   **Zhuh -<u>trah</u>-vy**
    Mondays.   *le lundi.*   **luh -<u>luhn</u>-dee**

Tuesdays.	*le mardi.*	luh -<u>mar</u>-dee
Wednesdays.	*le mercredi.*	luh -<u>mare</u>-cruh-dee
Thursdays.	*le jeudi.*	luh -<u>zhuh</u>-dee
Fridays.	*le vendredi.*	luh -<u>vehn</u>-druh-dee
Saturdays.	*le samedi.*	luh -<u>sahm</u>-dee
Sundays.	*le dimanche.*	luh -dee-<u>mehn</u>-sh

183.

January.	*le janvier.*	luh <u>zhehn</u>-vee-yay
February.	*le février.*	luh <u>fay</u>-vree-yay
March.	*le mars.*	luh marse
April.	*l'avril.*	lahv-<u>reel</u>
May.	*le mai.*	luh may
June.	*le juin.*	luh zhwehn
July.	*le juillet.*	luh <u>zhwee</u>-yay
August.	*l'août.*	<u>loot</u>
September.	*le septembre.*	luh say-<u>tahm</u>-bruh
October.	*l'octobre.*	lok-<u>toh</u>-bruh
November.	*le novembre.*	luh no-<u>vahm</u>-bruh
December.	*le décembre.*	luh day-<u>sem</u>-bruh

184.   Our appointment is for March 4th.
Notre rendez-vous est pour le quatre mars.
Note <u>rehn</u>-day-voo ay poor luh <u>kaht</u> marse

185.   Next month.   *Le mois prochain.*   **Luh <u>mwah</u> pro-<u>shihn</u>**

186.   Last month.   *Le mois dernier.*   **Luh mwah dare-<u>nyay</u>**

187.   My birthday is April 16th.
Mon anniversaire, c'est le seize avril.
<u>Mohn</u> ehn-ee-vair-<u>sair</u> say luh <u>sez</u> ahv-<u>reel</u>

TALKING ABOUT THE WEATHER AND SEASONS

188.   What's the weather like today?
Quel temps fait-il aujourd'hui?
Kell <u>tehn</u> fate eel oh-<u>zhoor</u>-dwee

189.   What's the forecast for tomorrow?
       Quelle est la météo pour demain?
       Kell ay lah <u>may-tay</u>-oh poor duh-<u>mihn</u>

190.   It's sunny.   *Il fait du soleil.*   Eel fay doo <u>soh-lay</u>

191.   It's cloudy.   *Le ciel est couvert.*   Luh see-yell ay <u>koo</u>-vair

192.   It's windy.   *Il y a du vent.*   Eel ya doo <u>vehn</u>

193.   It's cold.   *Il fait froid.*   Eel fay <u>fwah</u>

194.   It's hot.   *Il fait chaud.*   Eel fay <u>shoh</u>

195.   It's (very) chilly.   *Il fait (très) frais.*   Eel fay (tray) <u>fray</u>

196.   It's snowing.   *Il neige.*   Eel <u>nehzh</u>

197.   It's raining.   *Il pleut.*   Eel <u>pluh</u>

Chapter 2
Travel

TRAVEL: GENERAL VOCABULARY AND EXPRESSIONS

198. Excuse me, where is . . . ?   *Excusez-moi, où se trouve . . . ?*
     Ecks-kyoo-z-ay mwah oo suh troov

     . . . downtown.   . . . *le centre-ville.*   luh <u>sehn</u>-truh <u>veel</u>

     . . . the shopping district.
     . . . *le quartier / le centre commercial.*
     luh <u>kar</u>-tee-yay / luh <u>sehn</u>-truh ko-mer-see-<u>ahl</u>

     . . . the residential neighborhood.
     . . . *le quartier résidentiel.*   luh <u>kar</u>-tee-yay rez-ee-dehn-see-<u>yell</u>

199. Is this the right direction?
     Est-ce la bonne direction?   Ess lah <u>buhn</u> dee-rek-<u>syuhn</u>

200. Where is it?   *Où est-ce?*   Oo ess

201. To the right?   *À gauche?*   Ah <u>goh</u>-sh

202. To the left?   *À droite?*   Ah <u>dwaht</u>

203. Is it on this side of the street?
     Est-ce de ce côté de la rue?
     Ess duh <u>suh</u> koh-tay duh lah <u>roo</u>

204. Is it on the other side of the street?
     Est-ce de l'autre côté de la rue?
     Ess duh <u>lohte</u> koh-tay duh lah <u>roo</u>

205. Straight ahead?   *Tout droit?*   Too <u>dwah</u>

206. Forward.   *Avant / En avant.*   **Ah-<u>vehn</u> / Ehn ah-<u>vehn</u>**

207. Back.   *Arrière / En arrière.*   **Ah-ree-<u>yair</u> / Ehn <u>ah</u>-ree-<u>yair</u>**

208. In front of.   *En face de.*   **Ehn fahs <u>duh</u>**

209. Behind.   *Derrière.*   **Dare-ee-<u>yair</u>**

210. Next to.   *À côté de.*   **Ah koh-tay <u>duh</u>**

211. To the right of.   *À la droite de.*   **Ah lah <u>dwaht</u> <u>duh</u>**

212. To the left of.   *À la gauche de.*   **Ah lah <u>goh-sh</u> <u>duh</u>**

213. To the north.   *Au nord.*   **Oh <u>nor</u>**

214. To the south.   *Au sud.*   **Oh s<u>ood</u>**

215. To the east.   *À l'est.*   **Ah <u>lest</u>**

216. To the west.   *À l'ouest.*   **Ah luh-<u>west</u>**

217. What is the address?   *Quelle est l'adresse?*
      Kell ay lah-<u>dress</u>

218. What street is this?   *On est dans quelle rue?*
      Ohn ay dehn kell <u>roo</u>

219. Where is the nearest travel agency?
      Où est l'agence de voyage la plus proche?
      Oo ay lah-<u>zhens</u> duh voy-<u>ahzh</u> lah ploo <u>proh-sh</u>

220. Can you help me make a reservation?
      Pourriez-vous m'aider à faire une réservation?
      Poo-ree-yay voo <u>may</u>-day ah fair oon <u>ray</u>-zair-vah-<u>syion</u>

221. How long is the trip between . . . and . . . ?
      Cela prend combien de temps pour aller de . . . à . . . ?
      **Suh-lah <u>prehn</u> kum-<u>byehn</u> duh <u>tehn</u> poor ah-lay
      duh . . . ah . . .**

222. Where can I get a (train) schedule?
      Où puis-je trouver les horaires (de train)?
      Oo pwee zhuh troo-vay laze <u>or-air</u> (duh trehn)

223. Will I need my passport?
Est-ce que j'aurai besoin de mon passeport?
Ess kuh zhohr-ay <u>buh</u>-zwehn duh mohn pass-<u>por</u>

224. Do I need a visa to visit this country?
Est-ce que je dois avoir un visa pour visiter ce pays?
Ess kuh zhuh dwah <u>zahv-wahr</u> uhn vee-<u>za</u> pohr vee-zee-tay suh <u>payee</u>

225. I missed . . .   *J'ai manqué . . .*   zhay <u>mehn</u>-kay

    my flight.   *mon vol.*   mohn <u>vuhl</u>

    my train.   *mon train.*   mohn <u>trehn</u>

    my local bus.   *mon bus.*   mohn <u>boos</u>

    my intercity bus.   *mon car.*   mohn <u>kar</u>

    my shuttle.   *ma navette.*   mah nah-<u>vet</u>

    my ride.   *mon moyen de transport.*
    mohn mwa-<u>yen</u> duh trehn-<u>spore</u>

TICKETS

226. Ticket.   *Le billet.*   Luh bee-<u>yay</u>

227. First class.   *Première classe.*   <u>Pruh</u>-me-yair <u>klahss</u>

228. Second class.   *Deuxième classe.*   <u>Duh</u>-zee-yem <u>klahss</u>

229. A reserved seat.   *Une place réservée.*
Oon <u>plahs</u> ray-zair-<u>vay</u>

230. Discounted-rate ticket.   *Un billet à tarif réduit.*
Uhn bee-<u>yay</u> ah tah-<u>reef</u> ray-<u>dwee</u>

231. Group rate.   *Un tarif de groupe.*   Uhn tah-<u>reef</u> duh <u>groop</u>

232. Student discount.   *Un tarif étudiant.*
Uhn tah-<u>reef</u> ay-too-<u>dyehn</u>

233. Senior discount.   *Un tarif troisième âge.*
Uhn tah-<u>reef</u> twa-zyem <u>ahzh</u>

234. I need to go to the ticket counter.
J'ai besoin d'aller au comptoir.
Zhay <u>buh</u>-zwehn <u>dah</u>-lay oh con-<u>twahr</u>

235. How much does this ticket cost?
     Combien coûte ce billet?
     Kum-<u>byehn</u> koot suh <u>bee</u>-yay

236. Where is the ticket window?
     Où est le guichet?   Oo <u>ay</u> luh <u>gee</u>-shay

237. I'd like to buy a one-way ticket.
     Je voudrais acheter un billet simple.
     Zhuh voo-dray <u>ahsh</u>-tay uhn <u>bee</u>-yay <u>sihm</u>-pluh

238. I'd like to buy a round-trip ticket.
     Je voudrais acheter un billet aller-retour.
     Zhuh voo-dray <u>ahsh</u>-tay uhn <u>bee</u>-yay <u>ah</u>-lay-<u>ruh</u>-toor

239. I'd like a first-class ticket.
     Je voudrais un billet première classe.
     Zhuh voo-dray uhn <u>bee</u>-yay <u>pruh</u>-myair <u>klahss</u>

240. Is this ticket refundable?
     Est-ce un billet remboursable?
     Ess uhn <u>bee</u>-yay rahm-boor-<u>sahm</u>-bluh

241. Is it possible to change dates?
     Est-il possible de changer de dates?
     Et-eel puhs-<u>see</u>-b-luh duh <u>shehn</u>-zhay duh <u>daht</u>

242. Is it possible to have another seat?
     Est-ce que c'est possible d'avoir un siège différent?
     Ess-kuh say puhs-<u>see</u>-bluh <u>dahv</u>-wahr uhn see-<u>yezh</u>
     deef-fay-<u>rehn</u>

243. I would like a seat . . .   *Je voudrais un siège . . .*
     Zhuh voo-<u>dray</u> uhn see-<u>yezh</u>

     next to my husband.   *à côté de mon mari.*
     ah <u>koh</u>-tay duh <u>mohn</u> mah-<u>ree</u>

     next to my wife.   *à côté de ma femme.*
     ah <u>koh</u>-tay duh <u>mah</u> <u>fahm</u>

     next to the window.   *côté fenêtre.*
     <u>koh</u>-tay fuh-<u>net</u>-ruh

     next to the aisle.   *côté couloir.*   <u>koh</u>-tay <u>koo</u>-lwahr

244. Can I book a reservation on line?
Est-ce que je peux réserver en ligne?
Ess-kuh zhuh puh ray-zair-vay ehn lee-nyuh

245. Is this an e-ticket?   *Est-ce un billet électronique?*
Ess uhn bee-yay ay-lek-troh-neek

246. May I have a copy of my itinerary?
Puis-je avoir une copie de mon itinéraire?
Pwee-zhahv-wahr oon koh-pee duh mone ee-tin-ay-rair

TRAVELING BY CAR

247. A car.   *Une voiture.*   **Oon vwah-toor**

248. A car rental agency.   *Une agence de location de voitures.*
Oon ah-zhance duh low-kah-see-yon duh vwah-toor

249. I'd like to rent a car.   *J'aimerais louer une voiture.*
Zhem-ray loo-ay oon vwah-toor

250. What are your rates?
Quels sont vos tarifs?   **Kell sohn voh tah-reef**

251. Do I need to pay a deposit?
Faut-il verser un acompte?   **Foh-teel vair-say uhn ah-conte**

252. A driver's license.   *Un permis de conduire.*
Uhn pair-mee duh kuhn-dweer

253. Do I need an international driver's license?
Est-ce que j'ai besoin d'un permis de conduire international?
**Ess-kuh zhay buh-zwehn duhn pair-mee duh kuhn-dweer
ihn-tern-ah-syion-al**

254. Comprehensive insurance.   *L'assurance tous-risques.*
Lah-soo-rehnce too-rees-kuh

255. Does this price include comprehensive insurance?
Est-ce que ce prix comprend l'assurance tous-risques?
Ess-kuh suh pree kom-prehn lah-soo-rehnce too-rees-kuh

256. To drive.   *Conduire.*   <u>Kuhn</u>-<u>dweer</u>

257. I am driving from Sète to Pau.
     Je conduis de Sète à Pau.   Zhuh kuhn-<u>dwee</u> duh <u>set</u> ah <u>poh</u>

258. Do you have a map of the area?
     Avez-vous un plan de la région?
     Ah-vay-<u>voo</u> uhn <u>plehn</u> duh lah <u>ray</u>-zhee-on

259. Where is the nearest gas station?
     Où est la station-service la plus proche?
     Oo ay lah stah-<u>see-yion</u> sehr-<u>vees</u> lah ploo <u>proh-sh</u>

260. Fill it up, please.   *Le plein, s'il vous plaît.*
     Luh <u>plihn</u> see voo <u>play</u>

261. Can you check the air in the tires?
     Pouvez-vous vérifier la pression des pneus?
     Poo-vay voo <u>vay</u>-ree-<u>fyay</u> lah <u>press</u>-syion day <u>puh-nuh</u>

262. I need to have my car fixed.
     J'ai besoin de faire réparer ma voiture.
     Zhay <u>buh</u>-zwehn <u>duh</u> fare ray-pah-<u>ray</u> mah <u>vwah</u>-toor

263. My car has broken down.   *Ma voiture est en panne.*
     Mah <u>vwah</u>-toor ay tuhn <u>pehn</u>

264. I can't start the car.
     Je ne peux pas démarrer la voiture.
     Zhuh nuh <u>puh</u> pah <u>day</u>-mah-ray lah <u>vwah</u>-toor

265. The battery is dead.   *La batterie est à plat.*
     Lah <u>bah</u>-tree et ah <u>plah</u>

266. I am out of gas.   *Je suis en panne d'essence.*
     <u>Zhuh</u> swee zehn pehn dess-<u>ehnce</u>

267. I have a flat tire.   *J'ai un pneu crevé.*
     Zhay uhn <u>puh-nuh</u> kruh-<u>vay</u>

268. The engine is overheating.   *Le moteur chauffe.*
     Luh moh-<u>tuhr</u> shoh-ff

269. I think it needs water.   *Je crois qu'il lui faut de l'eau.*
     Zhuh <u>kwah</u> keel lwee <u>foh</u> duh <u>loh</u>

270. There is a leak.   *Il y a une fuite.*   **Eel ya oon fweet**

271. Is there a garage nearby?
Est-ce qu'il y a un garage près d'ici?
Ess keel ya uhn gah-razh preh dee-see

272. Can you tow me to the nearest garage?
Pouvez-vous me remorquer jusqu'au garage le plus proche?
Poo-vay voo muh ruh-more-kay zhoo-sk oh gah-razh luh ploo proh-sh

AIR TRAVEL

273. Airport.   *L'aéroport.*   **Lair-oh-pore**

274. How can I get to the airport?
Comment je fais pour aller à l'aéroport?
Kuh-muh zhuh fay poor ah-lay ah lair-oh-pore

275. Is this there a shuttle for the airport?
Il y a une navette pour l'aéroport?
Eel ya oon nah-vet poor lair-oh-pore

276. Airline.   *La compagnie de vol.*
Lah comb-pah-nee duh vuhl

277. I am flying on Air France.   *Je prends un vol Air France.*
Zhuh prehn uhn vuhl air-frehnse

278. Where do I check my bags?
Où est-ce que je peux enregistrer mes bagages?
Oo ess kuh zhuh puh ehn-ruh-zhees-tray may bah-gahzh

279. I'd like to confirm my reservation on . . .
J'aimerais confirmer ma réservation sur le vol . . .
Zhem-ray cone-feer-may mah ray-zair-vah-syion soor luh vuhl

280. Do I need a boarding pass?
Est-ce qu'il me faut une carte d'embarquement?
Ess keel muh foh oon kart duhm-bark-mehn

281. My flight is leaving at 7:45 in the morning.
Mon vol part à 7h45. (sept heures quarante-cinq)
Mohn vuhl pahr ah set-er-kah-rehn-sank

282. Is the flight late?
      Est-ce que le vol a du retard?
      Ess kuh luh <u>vuhl</u> ah doo ruh-<u>tar</u>

283. When is the next flight to Marrakech?
      Le prochain vol pour Marrakech, c'est quand?
      Luh proh-<u>shihn</u> vuhl poor <u>mah</u>-rah-kesh say <u>kehn</u>

284. Is this a direct flight?   *Est-ce un vol direct?*
      Ess uhn <u>vuhl</u> dee-<u>rekt</u>

285. How many bags can I check?
      Je peux enregistrer combien de bagages?
      Zhuh <u>puh</u> ehn-ruh-zhees-<u>tray</u> kum-<u>byehn</u> duh bah-<u>gahzh</u>

286. Where is the check-in for my flight?
      Où est l'enregistrement pour mon vol?
      Oo ay <u>luhn</u>-ruh-zhee-struh-<u>mehn</u> poor mohn <u>vuhl</u>

287. Where is the departure gate?
      Où est la porte d'embarquement?
      Oo ay lah <u>port</u> duhm-bark-<u>mehn</u>

288. Can I bring this on board?
      Je peux apporter cela à bord?
      Zhuh puh <u>ah</u>-pore-tay suh-lah ah <u>bore</u>

289. Where is the baggage claim?   *Où est le retrait des bagages?*
      Oo ay luh ruh-<u>tray</u> day bah-<u>gahzh</u>

290. Where is the luggage from the flight from . . . ?
      Où sont les bagages du vol en provenance de . . . ?
      Oo <u>sohn</u> lay bah-<u>gahzh</u> doo vuhl ehn pruhv-<u>nehnce</u> duh

291. We have jet lag.   *Nous souffrons du décalage horaire.*
      Noo soo-<u>frehn</u> doo day-cah-<u>lahzh</u> ore-<u>rair</u>

CUSTOMS AND BAGGAGE

292. Where is customs?   *Où est la douane?*   Oo ay lah <u>dwahn</u>

293. Where is the passport check?
      Où est le contrôle des passeports?
      Oo ay luh cone-<u>troll</u> day pass-<u>pore</u>

294. I'm here on a stopover on my way to . . .
     Je fais escale en route pour . . .
     Zhuh fay ess-<u>kahl</u> ehn root <u>poor</u>

295. My passport. *Mon passeport.* **Mohn pass-<u>pore</u>**

296. Here are my bags. *Voici mes bagages.*
     Vwa-see may bah-<u>gahzh</u>

297. I have nothing to declare. *Je n'ai rien à déclarer.*
     Zhuh nay ree-<u>ehn</u> ah <u>day</u>-klah-<u>ray</u>

298. This is for my personal use.
     Ceci est pour mon usage personnel.
     Suh-<u>see</u> ay poor mohn noo-<u>zahzh</u> pair-soh-<u>nell</u>

299. How much do I pay? *Je dois payer combien?*
     Zhuh dwah pay-<u>yay</u> kum-<u>byehn</u>

300. I'd like to leave these bags at the baggage office.
     Je voudrais laisser ces bagages en consigne.
     Zhuh voo-<u>dray</u> less-say say bah-<u>gahzh</u> ehn kuhn-<u>see-nyuh</u>

TRAVELING BY TRAIN

301. Train station. *La gare.* **Lah <u>gahr</u>**

302. Where is the train station? *Où se trouve la gare?*
     Oo suh <u>troov</u> lah <u>gahr</u>

303. When does the train for Calais leave?
     À quelle heure part le train pour Calais?
     Ah kell <u>er</u> par luh <u>trehn</u> poor <u>kah</u>-leh

304. The platforms are over there. *L'accès aux quais est là-bas.*
     Lahk-<u>say</u> oh <u>kay</u> ay <u>lah</u>-bah

305. Is this the right platform for the train to Brussels?
     Est-ce le bon quai pour le train pour Bruxelles?
     Ess luh bohn <u>kay</u> poor luh <u>trehn</u> poor broo-<u>sell</u>

306. Is this the train for Paris?
     Est-ce le train pour Paris?
     Ess luh <u>trehn</u> poor pah-<u>ree</u>

307. Is this the train from Paris?
Est-ce le train en provenance de Paris?
Ess luh <u>trehn</u> ehn pruhv-<u>nehnce</u> duh pah-<u>ree</u>

308. Does this train stop at Dijon?
Est-ce que ce train s'arrête à Dijon?
Ess kuh suh <u>trehn</u> sah-<u>rett</u> ah dee-<u>zhon</u>

309. Stamp your ticket.   *Composter votre billet.*
Kuhm-poh-<u>stay</u> vote bee-<u>yay</u>

310. What time does the train from Angers arrive?
Le train en provenance d'Angers arrive à quelle heure?
Luh <u>trehn</u> ehn pruhv-<u>nehnce</u> <u>dehn</u>-zhay ah-<u>reev</u> ah kell <u>er</u>

311. I'd like to buy a ticket on the TGV to Dijon.
Je voudrais réserver une place dans le TGV pour Dijon.
Zhuh voo-<u>dray</u> <u>ray</u>-zair-<u>vay</u> oon <u>plahs</u> poor <u>luh</u> tay-zhay-<u>vay</u>
poor dee-<u>zhon</u>

312. Is there a connection?   *Est-ce qu'il y a une correspondance?*
Ess keel <u>ya</u> oon <u>core</u>-ess-pehn-<u>dehnce</u>

313. How much time do I have to make the connection?
Combien de temps est-ce que j'ai pour prendre la correspondance?
Kum-<u>byehn</u> duh <u>tehn</u> es kuh <u>zhay</u> poor <u>prehn</u>-druh lah
<u>core</u>-ess-pehn-<u>dehnce</u>

314. We have two reserved seats.
On a deux places réservées.
Oh nah <u>duh</u> plahs <u>ray</u>-zair-<u>vay</u>

315. Tickets, please.   *Présentez vos billets, s'il vous plaît.*
<u>Pray</u>-zehn-tay voh bee-<u>yay</u> see voo <u>play</u>

316. This seat is taken.   *Cette place est prise.*
Sett <u>plahs</u> ay <u>preez</u>

317. Where is the dining car?
Où est le wagon-restaurant?
Oo ay luh <u>vah</u>-guhn ress-toh-<u>rehn</u>

318. Does this train have Wi-Fi?
Est-ce que ce train a une borne Wi-Fi?
Ess kuh suh <u>trehn</u> ah oon <u>born</u> wee-<u>fee</u>

TAKING THE BUS

319. Bus station. *La gare routière.* **Lah gahr roo-tee-air**

320. Intercity bus. *Le car.* **Luh kar**

321. I would like a schedule, please.
Je voudrais un horaire, s'il vous plaît.
Zhuh voo-dray uhn ore-rair see voo play

322. Local bus. *Le bus.* **Luh boos**

323. Bus stop. *L'arrêt de bus.* **Lah-ray duh boos**

324. A book of tickets, please.
Un carnet de tickets, s'il vous plaît.
Uhn kar-nay duh tee-kay see voo play

325. Is there a bus that goes to . . . ?
Est-ce qu'il y a un bus pour . . . ?
Ess keel yah uhn boos poor

326. Which route is it? *C'est quelle ligne?*
Say kell lee-nyuh

327. Where do I get the bus to go to . . . ?
Où est-ce que je prends le bus pour aller à . . . ?
Oo ess kuh zhuh prehn luh boos poor ah-lay ah

328. What time is the first bus?
C'est à quelle heure le premier bus?
Say ah kell er luh pruh-mee-yay boos

329. When does the last bus leave?
C'est à quelle heure le dernier bus?
Say ah kell er luh dare-nyay boos

330. Where is the nearest bus stop?
Où est l'arrêt de bus le plus proche?
Oo ay lah-ray duh boos luh ploo proh-sh

331. Does this bus stop downtown?
Est-ce que ce bus s'arrête au centre-ville?
Ess kuh suh boos sah-ret oh sehn-truh veel

332.   Can you please tell me where to get off?
       Pourriez-vous me dire où je dois descendre?
       Poo-ree-ay voo <u>muh</u> deer oo zhuh <u>dwah</u> duh-<u>san</u>-druh

333.   The next stop, please.
       Le prochain arrêt, s'il vous plaît.
       Luh proh-<u>shihn</u> ah-<u>ray</u> see voo <u>play</u>

334.   Will I need to change buses?
       Est-ce que j'aurai besoin de changer de bus?
       Ess kuh zhohre-<u>ay</u> <u>buh</u>-zwehn duh shehn-<u>zhay</u> duh <u>boos</u>

TAXI!

335.   Taxi stand.   *L'arrêt de taxi.*   **Lah-<u>ray</u> duh tack-<u>see</u>**

336.   Where can I get a taxi?
       Où est-ce que je peux trouver un taxi?
       Oo ess kuh zhuh <u>puh</u> troo-vay uhn tack-<u>see</u>

337.   Can you please call a taxi?
       Pourriez-vous m'appeler un taxi?
       Poo-ree-ay voo <u>map</u>-lay uhn tack-<u>see</u>

338.   Would you like to share a taxi?
       Voudriez-vous partager un taxi?
       Voo-dree-ay voo par-tah-<u>zhay</u> uhn tack-<u>see</u>

339.   How much is the fare into town?
       C'est combien pour aller en ville?
       Say kum-<u>byehn</u> poor ah-lay ehn <u>veel</u>

340.   I'd like to go to . . .   *Je voudrais aller . . .*
       Zhuh voo-<u>dray</u> ah-<u>lay</u>

       the airport.   *à l'aéroport.*   ah lair-oh-<u>pore</u>

       the train station.   *à la gare.*   ah lah <u>gahr</u>

       the bus station.   *à la gare routière.*
       ah lah <u>gahr</u> roo-tee-<u>air</u>

341.   I'm in a hurry.   *Je suis pressé(e).*   **Zhuh swee press-<u>say</u>**

342.   Is it far?   *C'est loin?*   **Say <u>lwehn</u>**

343. Here's the address.   *Voici l'adresse.*   Vwa-<u>see</u> lah-<u>dress</u>

344. Can you stop here, please?
Pouvez-vous arrêter ici, s'il vous plaît?
Poo-vay-voo ah-ret-<u>ay</u> ee-<u>see</u> see voo <u>play</u>

345. That's more than what's on the meter.
C'est plus qui est sur le compteur.
Say <u>ploos</u> kee <u>ay</u> serr luh comp-<u>terr</u>

346. I don't have any smaller bills.
Désolé, je n'ai pas de plus petits billets.
Day-zoh-<u>lay</u> zhuh nay <u>pah</u> duh ploo puh-<u>tee</u> bee-<u>yay</u>

347. Keep the change.   *Gardez la monnaie.*
Gar-<u>day</u> lah muh-<u>nay</u>

TAKING THE SUBWAY

348. Subway.   *Le métro.*   Luh <u>may</u>-troh

349. A subway ticket.   *Un ticket.*   Uhn tee-<u>kay</u>

350. Where is the closest subway station?
Où est la station de métro la plus proche?
Oo ay lah stah-<u>see-yion</u> duh may-<u>troh</u> lah ploo <u>proh-sh</u>

351. Where is the subway map?   *Où est le plan du métro?*
Oo ay luh <u>plehn</u> doo may-<u>troh</u>

352. Which line do I take to go to . . . ?
Quelle ligne de métro est-ce que je prends pour aller à . . . ?
Kell <u>lee</u>-nyuh duh may-<u>troh</u> ess kuh zhuh <u>prehn</u> poor ah-<u>lay</u> ah

353. I'd like a booklet of tickets, please.
Un carnet de tickets, s'il vous plaît.
Uhn kar-<u>nay</u> duh tee-<u>kay</u> see voo <u>play</u>

354. Is this the right direction for Montparnasse?
Est-ce la bonne direction pour Montparnasse?
Ess lah <u>bunn</u> dee-rek-<u>syion</u> poor mohn-par-<u>nahs</u>

355. What is the next stop?   *Quel est le prochain arrêt?*
Kell <u>ay</u> luh proh-<u>shihn</u> ah-<u>ray</u>

TRAVELING ON TWO WHEELS

356. Bicycle.   *Un vélo.*   **Uhn vay-low**

357. I'm planning on riding my bike this morning.
Je vais faire du vélo ce matin.
Zhuh vay fair doo vay-low suh ma-tihn

358. Do you have a helmet?   *Avez-vous un casque?*
Ah-vay-voo uhn kask

359. I'd like to rent a bike.   *J'aimerais louer un vélo.*
Zhem-ray loo-ay uhn vay-low

360. Are there bike paths?   *Y a-t-il des pistes cyclables?*
Ee yah teel day pees-tuh see-klah-bluh

361. Scooter.   *Une moto.*   **Oon mow-tow**

362. I'd like to rent a scooter.   *J'aimerais louer une moto.*
Zhem-ray loo-ay oon mow-tow

GOING ON FOOT

363. Can I get there on foot?
Est-ce qu'on peut y aller à pied?
Ess kohn puht ee ah-lay ah pee-yay

364. It's ten minutes away.   *C'est à dix minutes d'ici.*
Set ah dee mee-noot dee-see

365. Do you have a map of the neighborhood?
Avez-vous un plan du quartier?
Ah-vay-voo uhn plehn doo kar-tee-yay

366. Is there a guided walk that you recommend?
Y a-t-il des promenades guidées que vous recommandez?
**Ee yah teel day pruhm-nahd ghee-day kuh voo
ruh-kuh-mehn-day**

367. Do you have a guide to local walks?
Avez-vous un guide des promenades?
Ah-vay-voo uhn geed day pruhm-nahd

368. How long will this walk take?
Ça prendra combien de temps?
Sah prehn-<u>drah</u> kum-<u>byehn</u> duh <u>tehn</u>

369. We'd like to take a hike.
On voudrait faire une promenade/randonnée.
Ohn voo-<u>dray</u> fair oon pruhm-<u>nahd</u> / rehn-doh-<u>nay</u>

370. We'd like to go climbing.
On voudrait faire de l'escalade.
Ohn voo-<u>dray</u> fair duh <u>less</u>-kah-<u>lahd</u>

371. Do I need walking shoes?
Est-ce que j'aurai besoin de chaussures de marche?
Ess <u>kuh</u> zhohre-ay <u>buh</u>-zwehn duh shoh-<u>ser</u> duh <u>marsh</u>

372. Where are the hiking trails?
Où sont les sentiers de randonnées pédestres?
Oo sehn lay <u>sehn</u>-tee-yay duh rehn-doh-<u>nay</u> ped-<u>estre</u>

373. Is it a difficult climb?   *Est-ce que ça monte dur?*
Ess <u>kuh</u> sah mehnt <u>door</u>

374. Is it steep?   *Est-ce que c'est une pente raide?*
Ess <u>kuh</u> sate oon pehnt <u>red</u>

AT THE HOTEL

375. Can you suggest a good hotel?
Pourriez-vous suggérer un bon hôtel?
Poor-ee-yay <u>voo</u> <u>soog</u>-zhay-<u>ray</u> uhn bohn oh-<u>tell</u>

376. Can you suggest an inexpensive hotel?
Pourriez-vous suggérer un bon hôtel pas cher?
Poor-ee-yay <u>voo</u> <u>soog</u>-zhay-<u>ray</u> uhn bohn oh-<u>tell</u> pah <u>share</u>

377. Do you have a vacancy?
Avez-vous une chambre?   **Ah-vay <u>voo</u> oon <u>shahm</u>-bruh**

378. I'd like a double room.
Je voudrais une chambre pour deux personnes.
Zhuh voo-<u>dray</u> oon <u>shahm</u>-bruh poor <u>duh</u> pair-<u>sun</u>

379. I'd like a room for one person.
      Je voudrais une chambre pour une personne.
      Zhuh voo-<u>dray</u> oon <u>shahm</u>-bruh poor <u>oon</u> pair-<u>sun</u>

380. I'd like a room with two beds.
      Je voudrais une chambre avec deux lits.
      Zhuh voo-<u>dray</u> oon <u>shahm</u>-bruh ah-<u>vek</u> duh <u>lee</u>

381. I have a reservation under the name "Jones."
      J'ai une réservation au nom de "Jones."
      Zhay oon <u>ray</u>-zair-vah-<u>syion</u> oh nohm duh <u>Jones</u>

382. Where can I park the car?
      Où est-ce que je peux garer la voiture?
      Oo ess <u>kuh</u> zhuh puh <u>gah</u>-ray lah vwah-<u>toor</u>

383. For two nights.   *Pour deux nuits.*   Poor <u>duh</u> nwee

384. May I see the room?   *Je peux voir la chambre?*
      Zhuh puh <u>vwahr</u> lah <u>shahm</u>-bruh

385. Would it be possible to have another room?
      Est-ce que ce serait possible d'avoir une autre chambre?
      Ess kuh suh <u>sray</u> poh-<u>see</u>-bluh dahv-wahr oon <u>oht-ruh</u>
      <u>shahm</u>-bruh

386. Is breakfast included?   *Le petit-déjeuner est compris?*
      Luh <u>puh</u>-tee <u>day</u>-zhuhn-ay ay khum-<u>pree</u>

387. Does the room have . . . ?   *Est-ce que la chambre a . . . ?*
      Ess <u>kuh</u> lah <u>shahm</u>-bruh ah

      a shower?   *une douche?*   oon <u>doosh</u>

      a bath?   *une baignoire?*   oon ben-<u>whahr</u>

      a TV?   *une télé?*   oon tay-<u>lay</u>

      a high-speed Internet connection?
      une connexion Internet haut-débit?
      oon kuhn-eck-<u>syion</u> ihn-tair-<u>net</u> oh day-<u>bee</u>

      air conditioning?   *la climatisation?*
      lah <u>kleem</u>-ah-tee-zah-<u>syion</u>

388. May I have the key?   *Je peux avoir la clé?*
      Zhuh puh ahv-<u>wahr</u> lah <u>clay</u>

389. We'll be back after midnight.
      On sera de retour après minuit.
      Ohn <u>suh</u>-rah duh ruh-toor ah-<u>pray</u> mee-<u>nwee</u>

390. Will the door be locked?   *La porte sera fermée?*
      Lah port <u>suh</u>-rah fair-<u>may</u>

391. Will we need to ring the bell?   *On aura besoin de sonner?*
      Ohn ore-<u>rah</u> <u>buh</u>-zwehn duh sun-<u>nay</u>

Chapter 3
Mealtimes

How people talk about mealtimes differs among Francophone countries. In France, *les repas* (meals) consist of *le petit-déjeuner* (breakfast), *le déjeuner* (lunch), and *le dîner* (dinner), whereas in Québec *le déjeuner* (breakfast), *le dîner* (lunch), and *le souper* (dinner) are the principal meals of the day. Children in both countries will come home to *un goûter* (after-school snack), and, if as a traveler you find yourself feeling a bit hungry, by all means stop for *un casse-croûte* (a snack)!

TALKING ABOUT MEALTIMES AND EATING: GENERAL EXPRESSIONS

392. Breakfast. *Le petit-déjeuner.*
Luh <u>puh</u>-tee <u>day</u>-zhuh-<u>nay</u>

393. Lunch. *Le déjeuner.* Luh <u>day</u>-zhuh-<u>nay</u>

394. Dinner. *Le dîner.* Luh <u>dee</u>-nay

395. I'm (very) hungry. *J'ai (très) faim.* Zhay (<u>tray</u>) <u>fihm</u>

396. I'm not (very) hungry. *Je n'ai pas (très) faim.*
Zhuh nay <u>pah</u> (tray) <u>fihm</u>

397. Yes, just a little, thanks. *Oui, juste un peu, merci.*
Wee, <u>zhoost</u> uhn <u>puh</u> mare-<u>see</u>

398. It's delicious.   *C'est délicieux.*   Say <u>day</u>-lee-<u>syuh</u>

399. I'm vegetarian.   *Je suis végétarien(ne).*
Zhuh swee <u>vay</u>-zhay-tahr-ee-<u>ehn</u> / <u>vay</u>-zhay-tahr-ee-<u>yen</u>

400. I'm vegan.   *Je suis végétalien(ne).*
Zhuh swee <u>vay</u>-zhay-tahl-ee-<u>ehn</u> / <u>vay</u>-zhay-tahl-ee-<u>yen</u>

401. A food allergy.   *Une allergie alimentaire.*
Oon <u>ahl</u>-air-zhee <u>ah</u>-lee-mehn-<u>tair</u>

402. I'm allergic . . .   *Je suis allergique . . .*
Zhuh swee <u>zahl</u>-air-<u>zheek</u>

403. to peanut products.   *aux arachides.*
oh <u>zahr</u>-ah-<u>sheed</u>

404. to seafood.   *aux fruits de mer.*
oh <u>fwee</u> duh <u>mare</u>

405. I'm lactose intolerant.   *J'ai une intolérance au lactose.*
Zhay oon <u>ihn</u>-tow-lay-<u>rehns</u> ow lak-<u>tohs</u>

406. I'm on a diet.   *Je suis un régime.*
Zhuh <u>swee</u> uhn ray-<u>zheem</u>

DINING OUT

407. Can you suggest . . . ?   *Pouvez-vous suggérer . . . ?*
Poo-vay voo <u>soog</u>-zhay-<u>ray</u>

408. a good restaurant.   *un bon restaurant.*
uhn <u>bohn</u> ress-toh-<u>rehn</u>

409. something close by.   *quelque chose près d'ici.*
kell kuh <u>shows</u> <u>pray</u> dee-<u>see</u>

410. a cheap restaurant.   *un restaurant pas cher.*
uhn ress-toh-<u>rehn</u> pah <u>share</u>

411.   I like . . . cuisine.   *J'aime bien la cuisine . . .*
       Zhem <u>byehn</u> lah kwee-<u>zeen</u>

French.	*française.*	frehn-<u>say</u>
Regional.	*régional.*	<u>ray</u>-zhee-on-<u>nahl</u>
Italian.	*italienne.*	ee-tahl-<u>yen</u>
Spanish.	*espagnole.*	ess-pah-<u>nyole</u>
Moroccan.	*marocaine.*	mah-roh-<u>ken</u>
Indian.	*indienne.*	ehn-<u>dyen</u>
vegetarian.	*végétarienne.*	vay-zhay-tahr-ee-<u>yen</u>

412.   We're looking for . . .   *On cherche . . .*   Ohn <u>share-sh</u>

a café.	*un café.*	uhn kah-<u>fay</u>
a snack bar.	*une buvette.*	oon <u>boo</u>-vet
a bar.	*un bar.*	uhn <u>bar</u>
a restaurant.	*un restaurant.*	uhn ress-toh-<u>rehn</u>
a crêpe place.	*une crêperie.*	oon krep-<u>ree</u>
a bistro.	*un bistro.*	uhn <u>bee</u>-stroh
a tea room.	*un salon de thé.*	uhn sah-<u>lohn</u> duh <u>tay</u>
a deli.	*un traiteur.*	uhn tret-<u>ter</u>

413.   I'd like to reserve a table . . .
       383 voudrais réserver une table . . .
       Zhuh voo-<u>dray</u> ray-zair-<u>vay</u> oon-<u>tab</u>-luh

for two.	*pour deux.*	poor <u>duh</u>
for tonight.	*pour ce soir.*	poor suh <u>swahr</u>
for tomorrow night.	*pour demain soir.*	

       poor <u>duh</u>-mihn <u>swahr</u>

414.   May I see the menu, please?
       Je peux voir la carte, s'il vous plaît?
       Zhuh puh <u>vwahr</u> lah <u>kart</u> see voo <u>play</u>

415.   I'll have . . .   *Je prends . . .*   Zhuh <u>prehn</u>

       the tourist menu.   *le menu touristique.*
       luh muh-<u>noo</u> too-rees-<u>teek</u>

       the fixed-priced menu.   *le menu à prix fixe.*
       luh muh-<u>noo</u> ah pree <u>feex</u>

all-taxes-included price.   *la formule TTC.*
lah fore-<u>mool</u> tay-tay-<u>say</u>

416.   Enjoy your meal!   *Bon appétit!*   Bohn <u>ah</u>-pay-<u>tee</u>

417.   Thanks, same to you!   *Merci, à vous aussi!*
Mare-<u>see</u> ah voo zoh-<u>see</u>

418.   More . . . please.   *Encore . . . s'il vous plaît.*
Ehn-<u>korc</u> . . . see voo <u>play</u>
bread.   *du pain*   doo <u>pihn</u>
water.   *de l'eau.*   duh <u>loh</u>

419.   The bill, please.   *L'addition, s'il vous plaît.*
Lah-dee-<u>syion</u> see voo <u>play</u>

420.   Is the tip included?   *Le service est compris?*
Luh sehr-<u>vees</u> ay kuhm-<u>pree</u>

MENU: GENERAL ITEMS

421.   Bread.   *Le pain.*   **Luh <u>pihn</u>**

422.   Salt.   *Le sel.*   **Luh <u>sell</u>**

423.   Pepper.   *Le poivre.*   **Luh <u>pwahv</u>-ruh**

424.   Butter.   *Le beurre.*   **Luh <u>buhr</u>**

425.   Sugar.   *Le sucre.*   **Luh <u>sook</u>-ruh**

426.   Tap water.   *L'eau du robinet.*   **Loh duh <u>roh</u>-bee-nay**

427.   Mineral water (flat).   *L'eau plate.*   **Loh <u>plaht</u>**

428.   Sparkling water.   *L'eau pétillante.*   **Loh pay-tee-<u>yehnt</u>**

429.   With ice.   *avec des glaçons.*   **ah-<u>vek</u> day <u>glah</u>-sohn**

BREAKFAST

In France, breakfast tends to be a light meal, sometimes consisting of bread or a pastry and coffee. Note that if you're looking for that large cup of coffee so prevalent in the United States, you'll want to order *un café américain*—espresso diluted with hot water—as ordering *un café* will get you an espresso. Breakfast in Québec tends to have more in common with the hearty American breakfast.

430.   I'll have ...   *Je prends* ...   Zhuh <u>prehn</u>

a coffee.   *un café.*   uhn <u>kah</u>-fay

a regular coffee.   *un café américain.*
uhn <u>kah</u>-fay ah-mary-<u>kihn</u>

a decaf.   *un déca.*   uhn <u>day</u>-kah

tea ...   *un thé* ...   uhn <u>tay</u>

with lemon.   *au citron.*   oh see-<u>trohn</u>

with milk.   *au lait.*   oh <u>lay</u>

431.   Do you want ... ?   *Voulez-vous* ... ? *(formal)*
Tu veux ... ? *(informal)*   Voo-lay <u>voo</u>   Too <u>vuh</u>

Hot chocolate.   *Un chocolat chaud.*
Uhn <u>show</u>-koh-<u>lah</u> show

fruit juice.   *Un jus de fruits.*   Uhn <u>zhoo</u> duh <u>fwee</u>

orange juice.   *Un jus d'orange.*   Uhn <u>zhoo</u> dow-<u>rehnzh</u>

432.   I would like ...   *Je voudrais* ...   Zhuh voo-<u>dray</u> ...

some toast.   *du pain grille.*   doo <u>pihn</u> gree-<u>yay</u>

with jam.   *avec de la confiture.*
ah-<u>vek</u> duh lah <u>kehn</u>-fee-<u>toor</u>

with honey.   *avec du miel.*   ah-<u>vek</u> doo <u>myel</u>

some cereal.   *des céréales.*   day <u>say</u>-<u>ree</u>-yahl

an egg.   *un œuf.*   uh <u>nuf</u>

some fried eggs.   *des œufs au plat.*   day <u>zuh</u> oh <u>plah</u>

an omelet.   *une omelette.*   oon uhm-<u>let</u>

a soft-boiled egg.   *un œuf à la coque.*
uh <u>nuf</u> ah lah <u>kuk</u>

a cheese omelet. *une omelette au fromage.*
oon uhm-<u>let</u> oh fro-<u>mah</u>-zh

bacon and eggs. *des œufs avec du lard.*
day <u>zuh</u> ah-vek doo <u>lahr</u>

ham and eggs. *des œufs au jambon.*
day <u>zuh</u> oh zhahm-<u>bohn</u>

a yogurt. *un yaourt.* uhn yah-<u>oort</u>

breakfast pastries. *des viennoiseries.*
day <u>vyen</u>-wahz-uhr-<u>ree</u>

a croissant. *un croissant.* uhn <u>kwah</u>-sehn

a chocolate-filled croissant. *un pain au chocolat.*
uhn <u>pihn</u> oh <u>show</u>-koh-<u>lah</u>

a raisin bun. *un pain au raisin.* uhn <u>pihn</u> oh ray-<u>zihn</u>

APPETIZERS, LUNCH ITEMS, AND SALAD

433. We'd like to have a light meal.
On a envie de prendre un repas léger.
Ohn ah ehn-<u>vee</u> duh <u>prehn</u>-druh uhn ruh-<u>pah</u> lay-<u>zhay</u>

434. Soup. *La soupe.* Lah <u>soop</u>

435. Chicken soup. *La soupe au poulet.* Lah <u>soop</u> oh <u>poo</u>-lay

436. Vegetable soup. *Le potage / la soupe aux légumes.*
Luh pow-<u>tahzh</u> / lah <u>soop</u> oh <u>lay</u>-goom

437. French onion soup. *La soupe à l'oignon gratinée.*
Lah <u>soop</u> ah luh-<u>nyion</u> grah-tee-<u>nay</u>

438. Fish soup. *La bouillabaisse.* Lah <u>boo</u>-yah-<u>bess</u>

439. A plate of cold meat. *Une assiette anglaise.*
Oon ahs-<u>yet</u> ehn-<u>glez</u>

440. I feel like having . . . *J'ai envie de prendre . . .*
Zhay ehn-<u>vee</u> duh <u>prehn</u>-druh

a sandwich. *un sandwich.* uhn sehnd-<u>weech</u>

a ham sandwich.   *un sandwich au jambon.*
uhn sehnd-<u>weech</u> oh zhahm-<u>bohn</u>

a tuna sandwich.   *un sandwich au thon.*
uhn sehnd-<u>weech</u> oh <u>tohn</u>

a cheese sandwich.   *un sandwich au fromage.*
uhn sehnd-<u>weech</u> oh fro-<u>mah-zh</u>

441.   He / She will have . . .   *Il / elle prend . . .*   Eel / el <u>prehn</u>

quiche.   *de la quiche.*   duh lah <u>keesh</u>

a green salad.   *une salade verte.*   oon sah-<u>lahd</u> <u>vair</u>-tuh

MAIN COURSE

442.   I'm ordering . . .   *Je commande . . .*   Zhuh kuh-<u>mehnd</u>

some roast chicken.   *du poulet rôti.*   doo <u>poo</u>-lay row-<u>tee</u>

some grilled fish.   *du poisson grillé.*
doo <u>pwah</u>-suhn <u>gree</u>-yay

some salmon.   *du saumon.*   doo soh-<u>mohn</u>

443.   I like . . .   *J'aime bien . . .*   Zhem <u>byehn</u>

seafood.   *les fruits de mer.*   lay <u>fwee</u> duh <u>mare</u>

mussels.   *les moules.*   lay <u>mool</u>

crab.   *le crabe.*   luh <u>krahb</u>

shrimp.   *les crevettes.*   lay kruh-<u>vet</u>

lobster.   *le homard.*   luh <u>oh</u>-mar

oysters.   *les huîtres.*   lay <u>zweet</u>-ruh

444.   Pasta.   *Les pâtes.*   Lay <u>paht</u>

445.   Choice of vegetable.   *Légume au choix.*
Lay-<u>goom</u> oh <u>shwah</u>

446.   A vegetarian couscous.   *Un couscous aux legumes.*
Uhn <u>koos</u>-koos oh lay-<u>goom</u>

447.   Steak.   *Le bifteck.*   Luh beef-<u>tek</u>

448.   Rice.   *Le riz.*   Luh <u>ree</u>

FRUITS AND VEGETABLES

449.   A fruit salad.   *une salade de fruits.*
       oon sah-<u>lahd</u> duh <u>fwee</u>

450.   A green salad.   *une salade verte.*   oon sah-<u>lahd</u> <u>vair</u>-tuh

DESSERT

In France, a cheese course frequently is served either before dessert or in place of it. Putting together a good cheese plate or *plateau de fromages* is an art in itself, as the cheeses should represent a harmonious variety of texture, milk type, color, and regional origin.

451.   What desserts do you have?
       Qu'est-ce que vous avez comme dessert?
       Kess kuh voo <u>zah</u>-vay kuhm duh-<u>sair</u>

452.   May I see the cheese plate?
       Puis-je voir le plateau de fromages?
       Pwee-zhuh <u>vwahr</u> luh <u>plah</u>-toh duh fro-<u>mah-zh</u>

453.   Can you suggest . . .   *Pouvez-vous me suggérer . . .*
       Poo-vay-voo <u>muh</u> soog-<u>zhay</u>-ray

       a mild cheese?   *un fromage doux?*   uhn fro-mah-zh <u>doo</u>

       a blue cheese?   *un fromage bleu?*   uhn fro-mah-zh <u>bluh</u>

       a good regional cheese?   *un bon fromage régional?*
       uhn <u>bohn</u> fro-mah-zh <u>ray</u>-zhee-on-<u>nahl</u>

       a goat cheese?   *un chèvre?*   uhn <u>shev</u>-ruh

454.   chocolate cake.   *Du gâteau au chocolat.*
       Doo gah-<u>toh</u> oh <u>show</u>-koh-<u>lah</u>

455.   ice cream.   *De la glace.*   Duh lah <u>glahss</u>

456.   apple tart.   *De la tarte aux pommes.*   Duh lah <u>tart</u> oh <u>pum</u>

457.   chocolate mousse.   *De la mousse au chocolat.*
       Duh lah <u>moos</u> oh <u>show</u>-koh-<u>lah</u>

BEVERAGES

458.   Would you like to have a drink?
        Vous voulez boire quelque chose?
        Voo voo-lay <u>bwahr</u> kel-kuh <u>shows</u>

459.   The wine list, please.   *La carte des vins, s'il vous plaît.*
        Lah kart day <u>vihn</u> see voo <u>play</u>

460.   A pitcher of water.   *Une carafe d'eau.*   **Oon <u>kah</u>-rahf <u>doh</u>**

461.   A bottle of mineral water.   *Une bouteille d'eau minérale.*
        Oon boo-tay <u>doh</u> meen-ay-<u>rahl</u>

462.   Some lemonade.   *De la citronnade.*
        Duh lah <u>see</u>-troh-<u>nahd</u>

463.   Fruit juice.   *Un jus de fruit.*   **Uhn <u>zhoo</u> duh <u>fwee</u>**

464.   Some cider.   *Du cidre.*   **Doo <u>see</u>-druh**

465.   A glass of milk.   *Un verre de lait.*   **Uhn <u>vair</u> duh <u>lay</u>**

466.   Some iced tea.   *Du thé glacé.*   **Doo <u>tay</u> glah-<u>say</u>**

467.   A bottle of red wine.   *Une bouteille de vin rouge.*
        Oon boo-<u>tay</u> duh <u>vihn</u> roozh

468.   A bottle of white wine.   *Une bouteille de vin blanc.*
        Oon boo-<u>tay</u> duh <u>vihn</u> blehn

469.   A beer.   *Une bière.*   **Oon <u>bee</u>-yair**

470.   What draft beers do you have?
        Qu'est-ce que vous avez comme bière pression?
        Kess kuh voo <u>zah</u>-vay kuhm <u>bee</u>-yair press-<u>yion</u>
        a darker beer?   *plus foncée?*   **<u>ploo</u> fon-<u>say</u>**

471. What's the house cocktail?
      Quel est le cocktail de la maison?
      Kell ay luh <u>cock</u>-tel duh lah <u>may</u>-zuhn

472. A pre-dinner drink   *Un apéritif.*   Uhn ah-<u>pay</u>-ree-<u>teef</u>

473. An after-dinner drink.   *Un digestif.*   Uhn <u>dee</u>-zhes-<u>teef</u>

Chapter 4
Leisure Activities

SIGHTSEEING

Most French towns have a local *syndicat d'initiative* or *office du tourisme* (tourist office) that is an excellent resource for travelers. Don't hesitate to pay a visit, as the staff is usually eager to suggest local attractions, recommend interesting excursions, and provide you with helpful maps, brochures, and other useful information that will help you make the most of your time there.

474. Where is the nearest tourist office?
      Où est le syndicat d'initiative le plus proche?
      Oo ay luh sihn-dee-<u>ka</u> dee-nee-sia-<u>teev</u> luh ploo <u>proh-sh</u>

475. What local attractions do you recommend?
      Quels centres d'intérêts est-ce que vous nous conseillez?
      Kell <u>sehn</u>-truh dan-tair-<u>ay</u> ess-kuh voo noo <u>kon</u>-say-<u>yay</u>

476. We're interested in a guided visit.
      On s'intéresse à une visite guidée.
      Ohn sihn-tair-<u>ess</u> ah oon vee-<u>zeet</u> ghee-<u>day</u>

477. What are the hours of operation?
      Quelles sont les heures d'ouverture?
      Kell sohn laze <u>er</u> doo-vair-<u>toor</u>

478. How much is the entrance fee?
      Quel est le prix d'entrée?   Kell ay luh <u>pree</u> dehn-<u>tray</u>

479. Where can I buy tickets?
      Où est-ce qu'on peut acheter des billets?
      Oo ess kohn puh tah-<u>shtay</u> day bee-<u>yay</u>

480. I'd like two tickets for tonight's show.
J'aimerais deux places pour ce soir.
Zhem-<u>ray</u> duh <u>plahss</u> poor suh <u>swahr</u>

481. What time does it start/end?
Ça commence / finit à quelle heure?
Sah kuh-<u>mehnse</u> / fee-<u>nee</u> ah <u>kell</u> er

482. Is there a reduced ticket price for . . . ?
Est-ce qu'il y a un tarif . . . ?   Ess keel yah uhn tah-<u>reef</u>

seniors.	*troisième âge.*	<u>twah</u>-zyem ahzh
students.	*étudiant.*	ay-too-<u>dyehn</u>
children.	*enfants.*	ehn-<u>fehn</u>
the unemployed.	*chômeurs.*	show-<u>mer</u>
groups.	*groupe.*	<u>groop</u>

483. We'd like to visit . . .   *On aimerait visiter . . .*
Ohn em-<u>ray</u> vee-zee-<u>tay</u>

an art museum. *un musée d'art.* uhn moo-<u>zay</u> dar
the shopping district. *le quartier commercial.*
luh <u>kar</u>-tee-yay ko-mer-see-<u>ahl</u>

484. We'd like to see . . .   *On aimerait voir . . .*
Ohn em-<u>ray</u> vwahr

a concert. *un concert.* uhn kon-<u>sair</u>
a play. *une pièce de théâtre.*
oon pee-<u>yes</u> duh tay-<u>aht</u>-ruh
a movie. *un film.* uhn feem
an exhibit. *une exposition.* oon ex-poh-zee-syion
an opera. *un opéra.* uhn oh-pay-rah

485. We'd like to go . . .   *On aimerait aller . . .*
On em-<u>ray</u> ah-<u>lay</u>

to a nightclub. *dans une boîte de nuit.*
dehnz oon <u>bwaht</u> duh <u>nwee</u>
to a bar. *à un bar.* ah uhn <u>bahr</u>
to a movie. *au cinéma.* oh <u>see</u>-nay-<u>mah</u>

486. My kids and I would like to go . . .
Mes enfants et moi aimerions aller . . .
Maze ehn-<u>fehn</u> ay <u>mwah</u> em-ree-ohn ah-<u>lay</u>

to the zoo.   *au zoo.*   oh <u>zoh</u>

to a playground.   *sur une aire de jeux.*
soor oon <u>air</u> duh <u>zhuh</u>

to a garden.   *à un jardin.*   ah uhn zhar-<u>dihn</u>

to a pool.   *à une piscine.*   ah oon <u>pee</u>-seen

487. Would it be possible . . . ?   *Est-ce que ce serait possible . . . ?*
Ess kuh <u>suh</u> ser-ay poh-<u>see-bluh</u>

to go to a beach.   *d'aller sur une plage.*
<u>dah</u>-lay soor oon <u>plah-zh</u>

go to a park.   *d'aller dans un parc.*
<u>dah</u>-lay dehnz uhn <u>par</u>

go to a botanical garden.
d'aller dans un jardin botanique.
<u>dah</u>-lay dehnz uhn zhar-<u>dihn</u> boh-tah-<u>neek</u>

visit a cathedral?   *de visiter une cathédrale?*
duh vee-zee-<u>tay</u> oon <u>kah</u>-tay-dral

to go to a soccer game?   *aller à un match de foot?*
<u>dah</u>-lay ah uhn <u>match</u> duh <u>foot</u>

INTERESTS AND HOBBIES

488. I'm interested . . .   *Je m'intéresse . . .*
Zhuh <u>mihn-tair-ess</u>

in movies.   *au cinema.*   oh <u>see</u>-nay-mah

in architecture.   *à l'architecture.*   ah <u>lar-shee</u>-tek-toor

in modern art.   *à l'art moderne.*   ah <u>lar</u> mow-<u>dairn</u>

489. Are you interested in politics?
Vous vous intéressez à la politique?
Voo vooz <u>ihn</u>-tay-ray-<u>say</u> ah lah <u>poh</u>-lee-teek

490. I'm studying . . .   *J'étudie . . .*   Zhay-too-<u>dee</u>
painting.   *la peinture.*   lah <u>pihn</u>-toor
music.   *la musique.*   lah moo-<u>zeek</u>

| fashion. | *la mode.* | lah mode |
| photography. | *photographie.* | lah <u>pho</u>-to-grah-<u>fee</u> |

491. I like . . .   *J'aime . . .*   Zhem

sports.	*les sports.*	lay <u>spore</u>
reading.	*la lecture.*	lah lek-<u>toor</u>
knitting.	*faire du tricot.*	fair doo <u>tree</u>-koh
drawing.	*le dessin.*	luh <u>dess</u>-ihn
sculpture.	*la sculpture.*	lah <u>skoolp</u>-toor

SPORTS

492. Is there a place nearby where I can . . . ?
Est-ce qu'il y a un endroit près d'ici où je peux . . . ?
Ess keel yah uhn <u>uhn</u>-dwah pray dee-<u>see</u> oo zhuh <u>puh</u>

ski.   *faire du ski.*   fair doo <u>skee</u>

play tennis.   *jouer au tennis.*
zhoo-ay oh <u>ten</u>-nees

swim.   *nager.*   <u>nah</u>-zhay

go hiking.   *faire de la randonnée.*
fair duh lah <u>rehn</u>-doh-<u>nay</u>

go camping.   *faire du camping.*   fair doo <u>kahm</u>-ping

go mountain climbing.   *faire de l'alpinisme.*
fair duh <u>lal</u>-peen-<u>eez</u>-muh

go biking.   *faire du vélo.*   fair doo <u>vay</u>-loh

water ski.   *faire du ski nautique.*   fair doo <u>skee</u> noh-<u>teek</u>

play golf.   *jouer au golf.*   zhoo-ay oh <u>golf</u>

go ice skating.   *patiner.*   <u>pah</u>-teen-<u>ay</u>

HOUSES OF WORSHIP

493. I am . . .   *Je suis . . .*   Zhuh swee

Christian.   *chrétien. (m.)*   *chrétienne. (f.)*
<u>kray</u>-tyen / <u>kray</u>-tyen-nuh

Catholic.   *catholique.*   <u>kat</u>-oh-<u>leek</u>

Jewish.   *juif. (m.)*   *juive. (f.)*   zhweef / zhweev

Muslim.   *musulman. (m.)   musulmane. (f.)*
<u>moo</u>-zool-mehn / <u>moo</u>-zool-mehn-uh

atheist.   *athée.*   <u>ah</u>-tay

494.   Is there . . . nearby?   *Y a-t-il . . . près d'ici?*
Ee yah <u>teel</u> . . . pray dee-<u>see</u>

a Protestant church.   *un temple protestant.*
uhn <u>tahm</u>-pluh <u>proh</u>-tes-tehn

a Catholic church.   *une église catholique.*
oon <u>ay</u>-gleez <u>kah</u>-toh-<u>leek</u>

a synagogue.   *une synagogue.*   oon <u>seen</u>-oh-gog

a mosque.   *une mosquée.*   oon <u>moss</u>-kay

a religious site.   *un site religieux.*   uhn <u>seet</u> ruh-leezh-<u>yuh</u>

When is the service?   *Quelle est l'heure de l'office?*
kell ay <u>ler</u> duh low-<u>fees</u>

495.   Can I go inside?   *Est-ce qu'on peut entrer?*
Ess kohn <u>puh</u> ehn-<u>tray</u>

Chapter 5
Shopping

BANKING AND MONEY

496. Is there . . . nearby?   *Est-ce qu'il y a . . . près d'ici?*
Ess keel <u>yah</u> . . . pray dee-<u>see</u>

  A bank.   *Une banque.*   Oon <u>behnk</u>

  An ATM.   *Un distributeur/guichet automatique.*
  Uhn dee-stree-boo-<u>ter</u> / ghee-<u>shay</u> oh-toh-mah-<u>teek</u>

  An American Express office.   *Un bureau American Express.*
  Uhn <u>boo</u>-roh American Express

  A currency exchange.   *Un bureau de change.*
  Uhn <u>boo</u>-roh duh <u>shehnzh</u>

497. I'd like . . .   *Je voudrais . . .*   Zhuh voo-<u>dray</u>
  to change some money.   *changer de l'argent.*
  shehn-zhay duh lar-<u>zhehn</u>
  to cash a traveler's check.   *encaisser un chèque de voyage.*
  ehn kess-ay uhn <u>shek</u> duh voy-<u>ahzh</u>
  to withdraw some money.   *retirer de l'argent.*
  <u>ruh</u>-tee-ray duh lar-<u>zhehn</u>

498. May I please have . . . ?   *Est-ce que je peux avoir . . . ?*
Ess kuh zhuh puh ahv-<u>wahr</u>
  some change.   *de la monnaie, s'il vous plait.*
  duh lah muh-<u>nay</u> see voo <u>play</u>

smaller bills.   *des billets plus petits, s'il vous plaît.*
day bee-<u>yay</u> ploo <u>puh</u>-tee see voo <u>play</u>

SHOPPING

499.   I'd like to do a bit of window shopping.
J'aimerais faire du lèche-vitrine.
Zhem-<u>ray</u> fair doo <u>lesh</u>-vee-<u>treen</u>

500.   How much does this cost?   *Combien coûte ceci?*
Kum-<u>byehn</u> koot suh-<u>see</u>

501.   Where are the cash registers, please?
Où est la caisse, s'il vous plaît?   Oo ay lah <u>kess</u>, see voo <u>play</u>

502.   I'd like to pay . . .   *J'aimerais régler . . .*
Zhem-<u>ray</u> reg-<u>lay</u>

with cash.   *en espèces.*   ehn ess-<u>spess</u>

by check.   *par chèque.*   pahr <u>shek</u>

by credit card.   *par carte de credit.*
pahr <u>kart</u> duh cray-<u>dee</u>

503.   May I have the receipt?
Est-ce que je peux avoir le reçu?
Ess kuh zhuh puh ahv-<u>wahr</u> luh ruh-<u>soo</u>

504.   Is there . . . nearby?   *Est-ce qu'il y a . . . près d'ici?*
Ess keel <u>yah</u> . . . pray dee-<u>see</u>

a department store.   *un grand magasin.*
uhn <u>grehn</u> mah-gah-<u>zihn</u>

a clothing store.   *un magasin de vêtements.*
uhn mah-gah-<u>zihn</u> duh <u>vet</u>-mehn

a shoe store.   *un magasin de chaussures.*
uhn mah-gah-<u>zihn</u> duh shoh-<u>ser</u>

a stationery store.   *une papeterie.*   oon <u>pah</u>-pet-ree

a bookstore.   *une librairie.*   oon <u>lee</u>-brair-ee

a jewelry store.   *une bijouterie.*   oon <u>bee</u>-zhoot-ree a tobacconist.   *un tabac.*   uhn <u>tah</u>-bah

a bakery.   *une boulangerie.*   oon <u>boo</u>-lehn-zhree

a pastry shop.   *une patisserie.*   oon <u>pah</u>-tee-sree

a convenience store.   *une épicerie.*   oon <u>ay</u>-pee-sree

a supermarket.   *un supermarché.*
uhn <u>soo</u>-per-mar-<u>shay</u>

a deli.   *un traiteur.*   uhn tret-<u>ter</u>

an open-air market.   *un marché en plein air.*
uhn mar-<u>shay</u> ehn plen <u>nair</u>

a flower shop.   *une fleuriste.*   oon fler-<u>eest</u>

a flea market.   *un marché aux puces.*
uhn mar-<u>shay</u> oh <u>poos</u>

a dry cleaner.   *un pressing.*   uhn <u>pres</u>-sing

a Laundromat.   *une laverie automatique.*
oon lav-<u>ree</u> oh-toh-mah-<u>teek</u>

a camera store.   *un magasin d'appareils photo.*
uhn mah-gah-<u>zihn</u> dah-pah-<u>ray</u> pho-<u>to</u>

a newsstand.   *un kiosque.*   uhn kee-<u>yahsk</u>

a hair salon.   *un salon de beauté.*
uhn <u>sah</u>-lohn duh <u>boh</u>-tay

a hardware store.   *une quincaillerie.*   oon <u>kan</u>-ky-<u>ree</u>

505.   At the department store.   *Au grand magasin.*
Oh <u>grehn</u> mah-gah-<u>zihn</u>

506.   Where is the . . . department?   *Où se trouve le rayon . . . ?*
Oo <u>suh</u> troov luh ray-<u>ohn</u>

Clothing.   *Vêtements.*   <u>vet</u>-mehn

Shoes.   *Chaussures.*   shoh-<u>ser</u>

Housewares.   *Appareils ménagers.*
ah-pah-<u>ray</u> <u>may</u>-nah-<u>zhay</u>

Electronics.   *Appareils électriques.*
ah-pah-<u>ray</u> <u>ay</u>-lek-<u>treek</u>

Toys.   *Jouets.*   <u>zhoo</u>-ay

Cosmetics.   *Maquillage.*   <u>mah</u>-kee-yahzh

507. At the clothing store.
Au magasin de vêtements.
Oh mah-gah-<u>zihn</u> duh <u>vet</u>-mehn

508. I'm looking for something . . .
Je cherche quelque chose de . . .
Zhuh <u>share-sh</u> kel-kuh <u>shows</u> duh

bigger.	*plus grand.*	ploo <u>grehn</u>
smaller.	*plus petit.*	ploo <u>puh</u>-tee
less expensive.	*moins cher.*	mwehn <u>share</u>

509. May I try this on? *Je peux l'essayer?*
Zhuh puh <u>less</u>-say-<u>yay</u>

510. Where is the changing room?
Où se trouve la cabine d'essayage?
Oo suh troov lah <u>kah</u>-been <u>dess</u>-say-yahzh

511. Where can I buy . . . ? *Où peut-on acheter . . . ?*
Oo puht uhn <u>ahsh</u>-tay

a dress.	*une robe.*	oon <u>ro</u>-buh
a skirt.	*une jupe.*	oon <u>zhoo</u>-puh
pants.	*des pantalons.*	day <u>pehn</u>-tah-lehn
a shirt.	*une chemise.*	oon <u>shuh</u>-meez
a dress shirt.	*un chemisier.*	uhn <u>shuh</u>-meez-<u>yay</u>
an undershirt.	*un débardeur.*	uhn <u>day</u>-bar-der
a tie.	*une cravate.*	oon krah-<u>vaht</u>
pajamas.	*des pyjamas.*	day <u>pee</u>-zhah-<u>mah</u>
a nightgown.	*une chemise de nuit.*	oon <u>shuh</u>-meez duh <u>nwee</u>
gloves.	*des gants.*	day <u>gehn</u>
a winter hat.	*un bonnet.*	uhn <u>bohn</u>-nay
a winter coat.	*un manteau.*	uhn <u>mehn</u>-toh
a raincoat.	*un imperméable.*	uhn <u>ihm</u>-pair-may-<u>ab</u>-luh
boots.	*des bottes.*	day <u>but</u>
socks.	*des chaussettes.*	day <u>shoh</u>-set

a scarf.   *une écharpe.*   **oon <u>ay</u>-sharp**

a sweater. (France)   *un pull.*   **uhn <u>pool</u>**

a sweater. (Québec)   *un chandail.*   **uhn <u>shan</u>-dy**

512. At the shoe store.   *Au magasin de chaussures.*
Oh mah-gah-<u>zihn</u> duh shoh-<u>ser</u>

513. What shoe size do you wear?
Quelle est votre pointure?   **Kell ay <u>votc</u> pwehn-<u>toor</u>**

514. I wear size . . .   *Ma pointure est le . . . / Je fais du . . .*
Mah pwehn-<u>toor</u> ay / Zhuh fay doo

515. I'm looking for . . .   *Je cherche . . .*   **Zhuh <u>share-sh</u>**

sandals.   *des sandales.*   **day sehn-<u>dahl</u>**

sneakers.   *des baskets.*   **day bas-<u>ket</u>**

high heels.   *des escarpins.*   **daze <u>es</u>-car-pihn**

flip-flops.   *des tongs.*   **day tehn-g**

516. At the bookstore.   *À la librairie.*   **Ah lah <u>lee</u>-brair-<u>ee</u>**

517. I'm looking for a . . .   *Je cherche . . .*
Zhuh <u>share-sh</u>

book.   *un livre*   **uhn <u>leev</u>-ruh**

something in English.   *quelque chose en anglais.*
kell-kuh <u>shows</u> ehn ehn-<u>glay</u>

novel.   *un roman*   **uhn <u>row</u>-mehn**

guide book.   *un guide touristique.*
uhn <u>geed</u> too-rees-<u>teek</u>

an English-French dictionary.
un dictionnaire anglais-français.
uhn <u>deek</u>-syion-air ehn-<u>glay</u> <u>frehn</u>-say

children's book.   *un livre pour enfants.*
uhn <u>leev</u>-ruh poor <u>ehn</u>-fehn

graphic novel.   *une BD.*   **oon <u>bay</u>-day**

518. At the stationery store.   *À la papeterie.*
Ah lah <u>pah</u>-pet-ree

519. I'd like to buy . . .   *J'aimerais acheter . . .*
Zhem-<u>ray</u> <u>ahsh</u>-tay

a pen. *un stylo.* uhn <u>stee</u>-low

a pencil. *un crayon.* uhn <u>kray</u>-ohn

a pad of paper. *un bloc-notes.* uhn <u>block</u>-note

some envelopes. *des envelopes.* days <u>ehn</u>-vel-ohp

520. At the jewelry store. *À la bijouterie.* Ah lah
<u>bee</u>-zhoot-ree

521. I'd like to have this watch repaired.
Je voudrais faire réparer cette montre.
Zhuh voo-<u>dray</u> fair <u>ray</u>-pah-ray set <u>mohn</u>-truh

522. Do you have a battery for this watch?
Avez-vous une pile pour cette montre?
Ah-vay voo oon <u>peel</u> poor set <u>mohn</u>-truh?

523. I'd like to buy . . .   *J'aimerais acheter . . .*
Zhem-<u>ray</u> <u>ahsh</u>-tay

a gift. *un cadeau.* uhn <u>kah</u>-doh

a bracelet. *un bracelet.* uhn <u>brass</u>-lay

a ring. *une bague.* oon <u>bahg</u>-uh

some earrings. *des boucles d'oreilles.*
day <u>book</u>-luh dore-<u>ay</u>

a necklace. *un collier.* uhn <u>kull</u>-yay

524. At the tobacco shop. *Au bureau de tabac.*
Oh <u>boo</u>-roh duh <u>tah</u>-bah

525. A pack of cigarettes, please. *Un paquet de cigarettes.*
Uhn <u>pah</u>-kay duh <u>seeg</u>-ah-ret

526. A lighter. *Un briquet.* Uhn <u>bree</u>-kay

527. Some matches. *Des allumettes.* Days <u>ahl</u>-oo-met

528. At the bakery. *À la boulangerie.* Ah lah <u>boo</u>-lehn-zhree

529. I'd like . . .   *Je voudrais . . .*   **Zhuh-voo-<u>dray</u>**
a loaf of French bread.   *une baguette.*   **oon <u>bah</u>-get**
half a loaf of French bread.   *une demi-baguette.*
oon <u>duh</u>-mee-<u>bah</u>-get
some rolls.   *des petits pains.*   **day <u>puh</u>-tee pihn**
a loaf of whole-wheat bread.   *un pain complet.*
uhn <u>pihn</u> kuhm-<u>play</u>

530. At the pastry shop.   *À la patisserie.*
Ah lah <u>pah</u>-tee-sree

531. We'd like . . .   *On voudrait . . .*   **Ohn <u>voo</u>-dray**
two croissants.   *deux croissants.*   **duh <u>kwah</u>-sehn**
a chocolate croissant.   *un croissant au chocolat.*
uhn <u>kwah</u>-sehn oh <u>shoh</u>-koh-<u>lah</u>
a raisin bun.   *un pain au raisin.*   **uhn <u>pihn</u> oh <u>ray</u>-zihn**
some pastries.   *des patisseries.*   **day <u>pah</u>-tee-sree**
some cookies.   *des biscuits.*   **day <u>bees</u>-kwee**

532. At the supermarket.   *Au supermarché.*
Oh <u>soo</u>-pair-mar-<u>shay</u>

533. Where is the . . . section?   *Où se trouve le rayon . . . ?*
Oo suh troov luh <u>ray</u>-ohn
Cheese.   *Fromage.*   **fro-<u>mah-zh</u>**
Wine.   *Vin et spiritueux.*   **vihn ay <u>spee</u>-ree-too-uh**
Candy.   *Confiserie.*   **kuhn-<u>fee</u>-sree**
Meat.   *Viande.*   **vee-<u>ehn</u>-duh**
Fish.   *Poisson.*   **<u>pwah</u>-sohn**
Dairy.   *Produits laitiers.*   **<u>pro</u>-dwee <u>lay</u>-tee-ay**

534. At the flower shop.   *Chez le fleuriste.*   **Shay luh fler-<u>eest</u>**

535. I'd like to buy a bouquet of flowers.
J'aimerais acheter un bouquet de fleurs.
Zhem-<u>ray</u> ahsh-tay uhn <u>boo</u>-kay duh <u>fler</u>

536. I'd like a combination of flowers.
J'aimerais un bouquet de fleurs assorties.
Zhem-<u>ray</u> uhn <u>boo</u>-kay day <u>fler</u> ah-sore-<u>tee</u>

537. I'd like to send some flowers . . .
J'aimerais envoyer des fleurs . . .
Zhem-<u>ray</u> <u>ehn</u>-vwah-yay day <u>fler</u>

to this address. *à cette adresse.* **ah set ah-<u>dress</u>**
to this person. *à cette personne.* **ah set pair-<u>sun</u>**

538. I'd like a house plant. *J'aimerais une plante.*
Zhem-<u>ray</u> oon <u>plehn</u>-tuh

539. At the dry cleaners. *Au pressing.* **Oh <u>pres</u>-sing**

540. Do you have a laundry service?
Avez-vous un service de blanchisserie?
Ah-vay vooz uhn <u>sair</u>-vees duh <u>blan</u>-shees-<u>ree</u>

541. When will my things be ready?
Quand est-ce que mes affaires seront prêtes?
Kehn ess kuh <u>maze</u> ah-<u>fair</u> suhr-ohn <u>prett</u>

542. Can you iron these clothes?
Pouvez-vous faire repasser ces vêtements?
Poo-vay voo fair <u>ruh</u>-pass-say say <u>vet</u>-mehn

543. Can you shorten these pants?
Pouvez-vous raccourcir ce pantalon?
Poo-vay voo <u>rah</u>-koor-seer suh <u>pehn</u>-tah-lohn

544. Do you do mending?
Est-ce que vous faîtes des petites réparations?
Ess kuh voo <u>fet</u> day <u>puh</u>-teet <u>ray</u>-pahr-ah-syion

545. At the Laundromat. (France)
À la laverie automatique. **Ah lah <u>lahv</u>-ree <u>oh</u>-toh-mah-<u>teek</u>**

546. At the Laundromat. (Québec) *À la launderette.*
Ah lah <u>lohn</u>-dret

547. What coins do I need for these machines?
Quelles pièces faut-il pour ces machines?
Kell pee-<u>yes</u> foh-teel poor say <u>mah</u>-sheen

548. Where can I buy some detergent?
Où peut-on acheter de la lessive?
Oo puh-tohn <u>ahsh</u>-tay duh lah less-<u>eev</u>

549. Where can I dry my clothes?
Où est-ce que je peux faire sécher mon linge?
Oo ess kuh zhuh puh fair <u>say</u>-shay mohn <u>lihnzh</u>

550. At the camera store.   *Au magasin d'appareils photo.*
Oh mah-gah-<u>zihn</u> dah-pah-<u>ray</u> pho-<u>to</u>

551. I'm looking for . . .   *Je cherche . . .*   Zhuh <u>share-sh</u>
a digital camera.   *un appareil numérique.*
uhn ah-pah-<u>ray</u> noo-may-<u>reek</u>
film for this camera.
une pellicule pour cet appareil photo.
oon pay-leel-<u>kool</u> poor set ah-pah-<u>ray</u> pho-<u>to</u>
batteries for my camera.
des piles pour mon appareil photo.
day <u>peel</u> poor mohn ah-pah-<u>ray</u> pho-<u>to</u>
a point-and-shoot camera.   *appareil compact.*
ah-pah-<u>ray</u> kuhm-<u>pakt</u>
a DSLR camera.   *appareil reflex.*   ah-pah-<u>ray</u> <u>ruh</u>-flex

552. Will I need a different plug / adaptor?
Est-ce que j'aurai besoin d'une prise différente?
Ess kuh zhore-ay <u>buh</u>-zwehn doon preez <u>dif</u>-fay-<u>rehnt</u>

553. At the newsstand.   *Au kiosque.*   Oh kee-<u>yahsk</u>

554. A newspaper, please.   *Un journal, s'il vous plaît.*
Uhn zhoor-<u>nal</u> see voo <u>play</u>

555. Where are the English-language magazines?
Où sont les publications anglophones?
Oo sohn lay <u>poob</u>-lee-ka-syion ehn-glow-<u>phone</u>

556.   At the hair salon.   *Chez le coiffeur.*
       Shay luh <u>kwah</u>-foor

557.   I'd like to make an appointment.
       Je voudrais prendre un rendez-vous.
       Zhuh voo-dray <u>prehn</u>-druh uhn <u>rehn</u>-day-<u>voo</u>

558.   Do you take walk-ins?   *Vous prenez sans rendez-vous?*
       Voo pruh-nay <u>sehn</u> rehn-day-<u>voo</u>

559.   I'd like . . .   *Je voudrais . . .*   Zhuh voo-<u>dray</u>
       a haircut.   *une coupe de cheveux.*
       oon <u>koop</u> duh shuh-<u>vuh</u>
       a blow-out.   *un brushing.*   uhn <u>brush</u>-ing
       highlights.   *des mèches.*   day <u>mesh</u>
       just a shampoo.   *juste un shampooing.*
       zhoost uhn shamp-<u>pwehn</u>

MEASUREMENTS

560.   500 grams of . . .   *500 grammes de . . .*
       Sank-sehn <u>grahm</u> duh

561.   A kilo of . . .   *Un kilo de . . .*   Uhn <u>kee</u>-loh duh

562.   A half-kilo of . . .   *Un demi-kilo de . . .*
       Uhn <u>duh</u>-mee <u>kee</u>-loh duh

563.   A bottle of . . .   *Une bouteille de . . .*
       Oon boo-<u>tay</u> duh

564.   A half-bottle of . . .   *Une demi-bouteille de . . .*
       Oon <u>duh</u>-mee boo-<u>tay</u> duh

565.   A liter of . . .   *Un litre de . . .*   Uhn <u>leet</u>-ruh duh

566.   A glass of . . .   *Un verre de . . .*   Uhn <u>vair</u> duh

567. A slice of . . . (pizza)   *Une tranche de . . .*
Oon <u>transh</u> duh

568. A package of . . .   *Une boîte de . . .*   Oon <u>bwaht</u> duh

569. A piece of . . . (meat)   *Un morceau de . . .*
Uhn <u>more</u>-soh duh

570. A little bit of . . .   *Un petit peu de . . .*
Uhn <u>puh</u>-tee <u>puh</u> duh

571. A box of . . .   *Une boîte de . . .*   Oon <u>bwaht</u> duh

572. A handful of . . .   *Une poignée de . . .*
Oon <u>pwa</u>-nyay duh

573. A can of . . .   *Une boîte de . . .*   Oon <u>bwaht</u> duh

574. A dozen . . .   *Une douzaine de . . .*   Oon doo-<u>zen</u> duh

575. A jar of . . .   *Un pot de . . .*   Uhn <u>poh</u> duh

576. More . . .   *Encore . . .*   Ehn-<u>kore</u>

577. Less . . .   *Moins . . .*   Mwehn

578. That's enough.   *C'est assez.*   Set ah-<u>say</u>

COLORS

579. Blue.   *Bleu(e).*   Bluh

580. Green.   *Vert(e).*   Vair/vairte

581. Red.   *Rouge.*   Roozh

582. White.   *Blanc(he).*   Blehn/blehnsh

583. Purple.   *Violet(te).*   Vee-oh-<u>lay</u>/vee-oh-<u>let</u>

584. Black.   *Noir(e)*.   **Nwahr**

585. Brown.   *Marron*.   **Mah**-ron

586. Yellow.   *Jaune*.   **Zhoh**-nuh

587. Orange.   *Orange*.   **Or**-<u>ehnzh</u>

588. Pink.   *Rose*.   **Roze**

Chapter 6
Health and Well-being

If you are feeling under the weather while traveling, make your first stop *la pharmacie* (the pharmacy). The role of the pharmacy is quite different from the American counterpart, as people tend to first consult pharmacists for health issues before contacting their doctor. At the pharmacy, you'll be able to get advice and fill prescriptions, as well as buy over-the-counter medications. Note that unlike the United States, these medications aren't available in supermarkets. If you need after-hours attention, look for a *pharmacie de garde* or *pharmacie de nuit*. In France, pharmacies are easily recognizable by the neon-green cross that identifies them.

AT THE PHARMACY

589. Where is the nearest pharmacy?
Où se trouve la pharmacie la plus proche?
Oo suh troov lah far-mah-<u>see</u> lah ploo <u>proh-sh</u>

590. Is there a 24-hour pharmacy nearby?
Est-ce qu'il y a une pharmace de garde près d'ici?
Ess keel <u>yah</u> oon far-mah-<u>see</u> duh <u>gard</u> pray dee-<u>see</u>

591. Do I need a prescription?
Est-ce que j'ai besoin d'une ordonnance?
Ess kuh zhay <u>buh</u>-zwehn doon <u>ore</u>-dun-<u>nehns</u>

592. I don't have a prescription.
Je n'ai pas d'ordonnance.   Zhuh nay <u>pah</u> <u>dore</u>-dun-<u>nehns</u>

593. My prescription is from an American doctor.
      Mon ordonnance est faite par un médecin américain.
      Mohn <u>ore</u>-dun-<u>nehns</u> ay fet par uhn <u>made</u>-sihn ah-mary-<u>kihn</u>

594. Is this product appropriate for children?
      Est-ce que ce produit s'utilise pour les enfants?
      Ess kuh suh pro-<u>dwee</u> soo-tee-<u>leez</u> poor laze <u>ehn</u>-fehn

595. What are the potential side-effects of this?
      Quels sont les effets secondaires potentiels de ceci?
      **Kel sohn lay <u>zay</u>-fay <u>suh</u>-kuhn-dare poh-tahn-<u>see-ell</u> duh
      suh-<u>see</u>**

596. I'd like to buy . . .   *J'aimerais acheter . . .*
      Zhem-<u>ray</u> <u>ahsh</u>-tay

      some aspirin.   *de l'aspirine.*   **duh <u>lass</u>-pee-<u>reen</u>**

      some vitamins.   *des vitamines.*   **day <u>vee</u>-tah-<u>meen</u>**

      some bandages.   *des pansements.*   **day <u>pans</u>-mehn**

      some tissues.   *des mouchoirs.*   **day moo-<u>shwahr</u>**

597. I need . . .   *J'ai besoin . . .*   **Zhay <u>buh</u>-zwehn**

      a toothbrush.   *d'une brosse à dents.*   **doon <u>bruss</u> ah <u>dehn</u>**

      some toothpaste.   *du dentifrice.*   **doo <u>dehn</u>-tee-<u>frees</u>**

      some dental floss.   *du fil dentaire.*   **doo feel <u>dehn</u>-tare**

      some shaving cream.   *de la crème à raser.*
      duh lah <u>krem</u> ah <u>rah</u>-zay

598. I'm looking for some medication for . . .
      Je cherche un médicament contre . . .
      Zhuh <u>share-sh</u> uhn may-dee-kah-<u>mehn</u> <u>kohn</u>-truh

      a headache.   *le mal de tête.*   **luh <u>mahl</u> duh <u>tet</u>**

      pain.   *la douleur.*   **lah doo-<u>ler</u>**

      a cold.   *le rhume.*   **luh <u>room</u>**

      the flu.   *la grippe.*   **lah <u>greep</u>**

      allergies.   *les allergies.*   **laze <u>ah</u>-lair-<u>zhee</u>**

      a cough.   *la toux.*   **lah <u>too</u>**

      a bee sting.   *une piqûre d'abeille.*   **oon pee-<u>koor</u> dah-<u>bay</u>**

      cramps.   *les douleurs.*   **lay doo-<u>ler</u>**

599. I need . . .   *J'ai besoin . . .*   Zhay <u>buh</u>-zwehn

     some pills.   *de comprimés.*   duh <u>kohm</u>-pree-<u>may</u>

     a suppository.   *d'un suppositoire.*
     duhn <u>soo</u>-poh-zee-<u>twahr</u>

     a cream.   *d'une crème.*   doon <u>krem</u>

     tampons.   *de tampons.*   duh <u>tahm</u>-pohn

     feminine napkins.   *de serviettes hygiéniques.*
     duh <u>sair</u>-vee-et ee-zhen-<u>eek</u>

     condoms.   *de préservatifs.*
     duh <u>pray</u>-zair-vah-<u>teef</u>

600. I need to replace my contact lenses.
     J'ai besoin de faire remplacer mes lentilles.
     Zhay <u>buh</u>-zwehn duh fair <u>rahm</u>-plah-say may <u>lehn</u>-tee

601. What contact-lens solution do you have?
     Qu'est-ce que vous avez comme solution d'entretien pour lentilles?
     Kess kuh voo <u>zah</u>-vay kuhm <u>soh</u>-loo-syion <u>dehn</u>-truh-ti-<u>yen</u> poor <u>lehn</u>-tee

602. What kind of diapers do you sell?
     Qu'est-ce que vous avez comme couches?
     Kess kuh voo <u>zah</u>-vay kuhm <u>koosh</u>?

603. Do you sell baby wipes, too?
     Est-ce que vous vendez des lingettes aussi?
     Ess kuh voo <u>vehn</u>-day day lihnzh-<u>et</u> oh-<u>see</u>

604. Do you have baby bottles like this one?
     Est-ce que vous avez des biberons comme celui-ci?
     Ess kuh voo <u>zah</u>-vay day <u>beeb</u>-rone kuhm suh-lwee-<u>see</u>

605. Please show me what you have in the way of sunscreen.
     Montrez-moi ce que vous avez comme écran solaire.
     Mehn-tray <u>mwah</u> suh kuh voo <u>zah</u>-vay kuhm <u>ay</u>-krehn soh-<u>lair</u>

606. Do you have something with a stronger SPF?
     Avez-vous quelque chose avec une protection plus forte?
     Ah-vay voo <u>kel</u>-kuh <u>shows</u> ah-<u>vek</u> oon <u>proh</u>-tek-syion ploo <u>fort</u>

607. Do you have something for a sunburn?
Est-ce que vous avez quelque chose pour un coup de soleil?
Ess kuh voo <u>zah</u>-vay <u>kel</u>-kuh <u>shows</u> poor uhn <u>koo</u> duh <u>soh</u>-lay

SEEING A DOCTOR

608. I am (very) sick. *Je suis (très) malade.*
<u>Zhuh</u> swee (<u>tray</u>) mah-<u>lahd</u>

609. I need to see the doctor.
J'ai besoin d'une consultation.
Zhay <u>buh</u>-zwehn doon <u>kone</u>-sul-tah-<u>syion</u>

610. Where does it hurt? *Où avez-vous mal?*
Oo <u>ah</u>-vay-voo <u>mahl</u>?

611. I have . . . *J'ai . . .* Zhay
a headache. *mal à la tête.* mahl ah lah <u>tet</u>
a sore throat. *mal à la gorge.* mahl ah lah <u>gorzh</u>
an earache. *une otite.* oon <u>oh</u>-teet
a migraine. *une migraine.* oon mee-<u>gren</u>
a cold. *un rhume.* uhn <u>roohm</u>

612. I think I have the flu. *Je crois avoir la grippe.*
Zhuh kwah <u>ahv</u>-wahr lah <u>greep</u>

613. I have indigestion. *J'ai une indigestion.*
Zhay oon <u>ihn</u>-dee-zhess-<u>tyion</u>

614. I have a rash. *J'ai une eruption cutanée.*
Zhay oon <u>ay</u>-roop-syion <u>koo</u>-tehn-<u>ay</u>

615. My child is sick. *Mon enfant est malade.*
Mohn <u>ehn</u>-fehn ay mah-<u>lahd</u>

616. I need a doctor. *J'ai besoin d'un médecin.*
Zhay <u>buh</u>-zwehn duhn <u>made</u>-sihn

617. May I please speak to a nurse?
Est-ce que je peux parler à une infirmière?
Ess <u>kuh</u> zhuh <u>puh</u> <u>par</u>-lay ah oon <u>ihn</u>-fair-mee-<u>air</u>?

618. Please take me to . . . *Veuillez m'emmener . . .*
Vuh-<u>yay</u> <u>mehm</u>-nay

a hospital. *à l'hôpital.* ah <u>loh</u>-pee-<u>tahl</u>

the emergency room. *à la salle des urgences.*
ah lah <u>sahl</u> daze <u>oorzh</u>-ehns

a pharmacy. *à la pharmacie.* ah lah <u>far</u>-mah-<u>see</u>

a 24-hour pharmacy. *à la pharmacie de garde.*
ah lah <u>far</u>-mah-<u>see</u> duh <u>gard</u>

619. Does he need to go to the hospital?
Faut-il le transporter à l'hôpital?
Foh-<u>teel</u> luh <u>trehns</u>-pore-tay <u>ah</u> loh-pee-<u>tahl</u>

620. I'm having intestinal problems.
J'ai des problèmes intestinaux.
Zhay day proh-<u>blemz</u> ihn-tess-tee-<u>noh</u>

621. I have high blood pressure.
J'ai une hypertension artérielle.
Zhay oon ee-pair-<u>tehn</u>-syion ar-<u>tare</u>-ee-<u>el</u>

622. Where is the aide?
Où est l'aide-soignante?
Oo ay <u>led</u> swehn-<u>yehnt</u>

623. Will you need to draw blood?
Est-ce que vous aurez besoin de faire une prise de sang?
Ess kuh vooz <u>ore</u>-ray <u>buh</u>-zwehn duh fair oon <u>preez</u> duh
<u>sehn</u>

624. I am taking this medication.
Je prends ce médicament.
Zhuh <u>prehn</u> suh <u>may</u>-dee-kah-<u>mehn</u>

625. I am diabetic. *Je suis diabétique.*
Zhuh swee <u>dee</u>-yah-bet-<u>eek</u>

626. I am pregnant. *Je suis enceinte.* Zhuh <u>sweez</u> ehn-<u>sihnt</u>

627. I am allergic to aspirin.
Je suis allergique à l'aspirine.
Zhuh sweez <u>ah</u>-lair-<u>zheek</u> ah <u>lahs</u>-pee-<u>reen</u>

628. I'm on the pill.   *Je prends la pilule.*
     Zhuh <u>prehn</u> lah <u>pee</u>-lool

629. I need antibiotics.   *J'ai besoin d'antibiotiques.*
     Zhay <u>buh</u>-zwehn <u>dan-tee</u>-bee-oh-<u>teek</u>

630. Is it serious?   *C'est grave?*   Say <u>grav</u>

631. How are you feeling?   *Comment vous sentez–vous?*
     Kuh-muh voo <u>sehn</u>-tay <u>voo</u>

632. I'm feeling better, thanks.   *Je vais mieux, merci.*
     Zhuh vay <u>myuh</u> mare-<u>see</u>

633. I don't feel well.   *Je me sens mal.*   Zhuh <u>muh</u> sehn <u>mahl</u>

634. I'm feeling dizzy.   *J'ai la tête qui tourne.*
     Zhay lah <u>tet</u> kee <u>toor</u>-nuh

635. I feel like throwing up.
     Je suis sur le point de vomir.
     Zhuh <u>swee</u> soor luh <u>pwehn</u> duh <u>voh</u>-meer

636. The situation is getting worse.   *La situation s'empire.*
     Lah <u>see</u>-too-ah-<u>syion</u> sehm-<u>peer</u>

637. I'm resting.   *Je me repose.*   <u>Zhuh</u> muh ruh-<u>poze</u>

638. May I have a receipt for my health insurance?
     Il me faut un reçu pour l'assurance.
     Eel muh <u>foh</u> uhn <u>ruh</u>-soo poor <u>lass</u>-oo-<u>rehns</u>

SEEING A DENTIST

639. Can you recommend a good dentist?
     Pouvez-vous recommander un bon dentiste?
     Poo-vay voo <u>ruh</u>-koh-mehn-<u>day</u> uhn <u>bohn</u> dehn-<u>teest</u>

640. I have a toothache.   *J'ai mal aux dents.*
     Zhay <u>mahl</u> oh <u>dehn</u>

641. Do I have a cavity?   *Est-ce que j'ai une carie?*
     Ess kuh <u>zhay</u> oon <u>kah</u>-ree

642. I think I have an abcess.   *Je crois avoir un abcès.*
Zhuh <u>kwah</u> ahv-<u>wahr</u> uhn <u>ahb</u>-say

643. I think I lost a crown.   *Je crois avoir perdu une couronne.*
Zhuh <u>kwah</u> ahv-<u>wahr</u> pair-dew oon koo-<u>run</u>

644. It hurts!   *Ça fait mal!*   Sah fay <u>mahl</u>

645. Can you . . . ?   *Pouvez-vous . . . ?*   Poo-vay <u>voo</u>
give me a filling.   *me faire un plombage.*
muh fair uhn <u>plohm</u>-bahzh

give me a temporary filling.
me faire un plombage momentané.
muh fair uhn <u>plohm</u>-bahzh <u>moh</u>-mehn-tah-<u>nay</u>

give me something for the pain.
me donner quelque chose contre la douleur.
muh duh-<u>nay</u> kel-kuh <u>shows</u> kone-truh lah dool-<u>er</u>

646. Does it need to be pulled?   *Faut-il l'arracher?*
Foh-teel <u>lah</u>-rah-<u>shay</u>

647. I need to have my dentures fixed.
J'ai besoin de faire réparer mon dentier.
Zhay <u>buh</u>-zwehn duh <u>fair</u> ray-pah-<u>ray</u> moh <u>dent</u>-yay

648. He/she wears braces.
Il/elle porte un appareil dentaire.
Eel / ell <u>port</u> uhn <u>ah</u>-pah-<u>ray</u> dehn-<u>tair</u>

Chapter 7
Communications

THE POST OFFICE

649. Where is the nearest post office?
Où est le bureau de poste le plus proche?
Oo ay luh boo-roh duh pust luh ploo proh-sh

650. Is there a mailbox nearby?
Il y a une boîte aux lettres près d'ici?
Eel yah oon bwaht oh lett-ruh pray dee-see

651. I need to mail . . .   *J'ai besoin d'envoyer . . .*
Zhay buh-zwehn dehn-vwah-yay

a letter.   *une lettre.*   **oon lett-ruh**

a postcard.   *une carte postale.*   **oon kart poh-stahl**

a money order.   *un mandat.*   **uhn mehn-dah**

a package.   *un colis.*   **uhn koh-lee**

652. I'd like to buy some stamps.   *J'aimerais acheter des timbres.*
Zhem-ray ahsh-tay day tihm-bruh

653. I need to send a registered letter.
J'ai besoin d'envoyer une lettre recommandée.
Zhay buh-zhwehn dehnv-wyah-yay oon lett-ruh ruh-koh-mehn-day

654. What's the postage for the U.S.?
C'est combien pour les États-Unis?
Say kuhm-byehn poor laze ay-tahz oo-nee

THE TELEPHONE

655. Where can I make a phone call?
      Où est-ce que je peux donner un coup de fil?
      Oo ess kuh zhuh <u>puh</u> duhn-<u>nay</u> uhn <u>koo</u> duh <u>feel</u>

656. How much does it cost to call the U.S.?
      C'est combien pour appeler les États-Unis?
      Say kuhm-<u>byehn</u> poor <u>ahp</u>-lay <u>laze</u> ay-tahz oo-<u>nee</u>

657. I'd like to buy a phone card, please.
      Une télécarte, s'il vous plaît.
      Oon <u>tay</u>-lay-<u>kart</u>, see voo <u>play</u>

658. Do you have a phonebook?
      Avez-vous un annuaire?
      Ah-vay <u>voo</u> uhn ah-noo-<u>air</u>

659. I'd like to phone home.
      Je voudrais appeler chez moi.
      Zhuh voo-<u>dray</u> <u>ahp</u>-lay <u>shay</u> mwah

660. I'd like to make a collect call.
      J'aimerais appeler en pcv.
      Zhem-<u>ray</u> <u>ahp</u>-lay ehn <u>pay</u>-say-vay

661. What is the number here?
      Quel est le numéro de téléphone ici?
      <u>Kel</u> ay luh <u>noo</u>-may-<u>roh</u> duh <u>tay</u>-lay-fun ee-<u>see</u>

662. Do you have the number for the American consulate?
      Avez-vous le numéro de telephone pour le consulat américain?
      Ah-vay <u>voo</u> luh noo-may-<u>roh</u> duh tay-lay-fun por luh <u>kohn</u>-suh-lah ah-mary-<u>kihn</u>

663. I'd like to buy a cell phone.
      J'aimerais acheter un téléphone portable.
      Zhem-<u>ray</u> <u>ahsh</u>-tay uhn <u>tay</u>-lay-fun por-<u>tahb</u>-luh

664. Is there a contract?
      Y a-t-il un contrat?
      Ee yah-teel uhn kohn-<u>trah</u>

665. My number is . . .   *Mon numéro est le . . .*
Mohn noo-may-<u>roh</u> ay luh

666. I'd like to speak to . . .   *Je voudrais parler à . . .*
Zhuh voo-<u>dray</u> pah-<u>lay</u> ah

667. Hello?   *Âllo?*   **Ah-<u>loh</u>**

668. Who is calling?   *C'est de la part de qui?*
Say <u>duh</u> lah <u>par</u> duh <u>kee</u>

669. It's Bruce calling.   *C'est Bruce à l'appareil.*
Say <u>Bruce</u> ah <u>lah</u>-par-<u>ay</u>.

670. I'll put you through to him/her.
Je vous le/la passe.
<u>Zhuh</u> voo <u>luh</u>/<u>lah</u> pass

671. One moment, please.
Un instant, s'il vous plaît.
Uhn ihn-<u>stehn</u> see voo <u>play</u>

672. Please hold on.
Patientez, s'il vous plaît.
Pass-yen-<u>tay</u> see voo <u>play</u>

673. Can you call back?
Vous pouvez rappeller?
Voo poo-vay <u>rahp</u>-lay

674. It's busy.   *C'est occupé.*   **Say <u>oh</u>-koo-<u>pay</u>**

675. Would you like to leave a message?
Voulez-vous laisser un message?
Voo-lay <u>voo</u> les-<u>say</u> uhn mess-<u>ahzh</u>

676. I'll call back later.   *Je vais rappeler plus tard.*
Zhuh vay <u>rahp</u>-lay ploo <u>tar</u>

677. We were cut off.   *Nous avons été coupés.*
Nooz ahv-uhn <u>ay</u>-tay <u>koo</u>-pay

678. I can't get the call to go through.
Je ne peux pas avoir le numéro.
Zhuh nuh <u>puh</u> pah <u>ahv</u>-wahr luh <u>noo</u>-may-roh

THE INTERNET AND COMPUTERS

679. A computer.   *Un ordinateur.*   **Uhn <u>or</u>-dee-nah-<u>tuhr</u>**

680. A printer.   *Une imprimante.*   **Oon <u>ihm</u>-pree-<u>mehnte</u>**

681. An ink cartridge.   *Une cartouche d'encre.*
      Oon <u>kar</u>-toosh <u>dehn</u>-kruh

682. A laptop.   *Un ordinateur portable.*
      Uhn <u>or</u>-dee-nah-<u>tuhr</u> por-<u>tah</u>-bluh

683. A battery.   *Une pile.*   **Oon <u>peel</u>**

684. A battery charger.
      Un chargeur pour piles.
      Uhn shar-<u>zher</u> poor <u>peel</u>

685. A power cord.   *Un cordon.*
      Uhn kore-<u>dohn</u>

686. A cable.   *Un câble.*   **Uhn ka-bluh**

687. Where can I get a Wi-Fi connection?
      Où je peux me connecter en Wi-Fi?
      Oo zhuh <u>puh</u> muh <u>kuhn</u>-ek-<u>tay</u> ehn <u>wee</u>-fee

688. Is there an Internet café nearby?
      Il y a un cyber café près d'ici?
      Eel <u>yah</u> uhn <u>see</u>-bair <u>kah</u>-fay pray dee-<u>see</u>

689. Can I go online?
      Je peux aller en ligne?
      Zhuh puh <u>ah</u>-lay ehn <u>lee</u>-nyuh

690. Do you have a high-speed Internet connection?
      Vous avez une connexion Internet haut-débit?
      Voo <u>zah</u>-vay <u>oon</u> koh-nex-<u>syion</u> ihn-tair-<u>net</u> oh-day-<u>bee</u>

691. Is there a computer I can use?
      Est-ce qu'il y a un ordinateur que je peux utiliser?
      **Ess keel <u>yah</u> uhn <u>ore</u>-dee-nah-<u>tuhr</u> kuh zhuh <u>puh</u>
      oo-tee-lee-<u>zay</u>**

692. Do you have a laptop?
      Vous avez un ordinateur portable?
      Vooz <u>ah</u>-vay uhn <u>ore</u>-dee-nah-<u>tuhr</u> pore-<u>tah</u>-bluh

693. Does this computer have an Internet connection?
      Est-ce que cet ordinateur a une connexion Internet?
      Ess <u>kuh</u> set <u>ore</u>-dee-nah-<u>tuhr</u> ah <u>oon</u> koh-nex-<u>syion</u>
      ihn-tair-<u>net</u>

694. I'd like to send an email.
      Je voudrais envoyer un mail.
      Zhuh voo-<u>dray</u> <u>ehn</u>-vwah-<u>yay</u> uhn <u>mel</u>

695. Do you have a website?
      Vous avez un site Internet?
      Vooz <u>ah</u>-vay uhn <u>seet</u> ihn-tair-<u>net</u>

696. Free Internet access.   *Accès Internet gratuit.*
      <u>Ax</u>-say ihn-tair-<u>net</u> grah-<u>twee</u>

697. Free Wi-Fi.   *Le Wi-Fi gratuit.*   **Luh** <u>wee</u>-fee grah-<u>twee</u>

698. I need to print a document.
      Je dois imprimer un document.
      Zhuh dwahz <u>ihm</u>-pree-may uhn <u>doh</u>-cue-<u>mehn</u>

699. I need to download some software.
      Je dois télécharger un logiciel.
      Zhuh dwah <u>tay</u>-lay-<u>shahr</u>-zhay uhn <u>loh</u>-zhee-<u>syel</u>

700. I need to save a file.
      Je dois sauvegarder un fichier.
      Zhuh dwah <u>sohv</u>-gar-day uhn <u>feesh</u>-yay

701. Can I plug in my USB flash drive?
      Je peux brancher ma clé USB?
      Zhuh puh <u>brehn</u>-shay mah <u>klay</u> oo-ess-<u>bay</u>

702. Can I log on?   *Je peux ouvrir une session?*
      Zhuh puh <u>oov</u>-reer oon <u>sess</u>-yion

703. I forgot my password.
      J'ai oublié mon mot de passe.
      Zhay <u>oob</u>-lee-<u>yay</u> mohn <u>moh</u> duh <u>pass</u>

704. Can I send a fax?   *Je peux envoyer un fax?*
     Zhuh puh <u>ehn</u>-vwah-<u>yay</u> uhn <u>fax</u>

705. I'd like to photocopy some documents.
     Je voudrais photocopier des documents.
     Zhuh voo-<u>dray</u> pho-to-<u>cop</u>-yay day <u>doh</u>-cue-<u>mehn</u>

Acknowledgments

I would like to thank those who have assisted me with this project, directly and indirectly. I gratefully acknowledge Rochelle Kronzek and Janet Kopito, editors at Dover Publications, Inc., for the opportunity to create a book helping French-language learners; Sandrine Siméon, for proofreading the phrases and making them as Frenchified as possible; Meredith Doran, for friendship and fulfilling dialogue about language learning and teaching; Bénédicte Monicat, for being a kind and encouraging colleague; the students at Penn State University, who continue to teach me so much; Barbara Campbell Hall, for her friendship and sly wit; my Tweeps, for keeping this Minnesotan's English as standard as possible; and my parents, Bob and Margaret McCoy, whose deep commitment to their own personal interests has always inspired me.

Index